GOOSEBERRIES

With lots love
+ thanks for
everything

Wendy. xxxx

Wendy Wright

•

GOOSEBERRIES

A story of a child's experiences at
boarding school in the post war years

Urchin Books
1992

Published in 1992 by Urchin Books
20 Douglas Road, Chingford, Essex E4 6DA

© Copyright Wendy Wright 1991
Cover picture by Ludovic Fealy

ISBN 0-9519014-0-0

Electronically composed in Bookman Light 10/13pt by
Scriptmate Editions

Printed on re-tree economy paper by
Booksprint,
31 Clerkenwell Close, London EC1

For Simon Reeve
and the children of Leyton

Other published writing by the author:

Edited and wrote introduction and teaching notes for *The Talisman,* a collection of poems and short stories by Ganga P Vimal (Translated from the Hindi and published by Forest Books)

Short stories:
Forest Writers Lit. Magazine
Roundabout Lit. Magazine

Extracts from books and short stories:
Speak English, an Eastern European Magazine published in Romania

Contents

Snapshots

It isn't there any more. I went and had a look a couple of years ago. The name was still there and the familiar line of elm trees, but that was all. A new low building stood in its place and a shiny board with neat white lettering. But the memory was so strong that it totally overpowered the featureless pile of small pink bricks and small square windows. I looked straight through those walls and into the past. This curious building looked so frail and insubstantial I felt I could stretch out my hand and rub it out, or crumble it in my fingers like a sand pie. The past streamed through solid and sturdy, set with figures half turning, mouths open to form a word caught at an instant and framed forever.

I was drawn in and drawn back into a never changing timescape where the people and events repeated themselves endlessly. And I tick-tock back and forth from the past to the present from the present to the past. Long ago all childhood feeling had dried hard enough to finger. Now the substance of those sensations, barely formed sensibilities of the past, the present and the intervening years have clarified into some recognisable formation.

How true is my truth? I don't know, I am the last person to judge, so much of my existence has been the fancy dress of fantasy anyway. Whether it's all true or not hardly matters, it's what I carry around in my crammed full trunk of experiences in the back of my mind.

The houses aren't there anymore, so I can't go back and knock on that huge oak door. Even if I could I couldn't check if this was still there and that was as I remember it.

Wars have started and ended since then, presidents have been assassinated. Whole epochs have exploded, sending out great showers of sparks that have reduced those little grey postwar days to cinders.

The trees were still there though, that short avenue of elms. A high dark canopy where only cracks of sky broke through.

It must have been a back door or tradesman's entrance that led to this corridor of trunks and fence that slid secretly down to the gate.

I ran my fingers along the grooves of the bark as I had done a hundred times before.

I was very young and very small when I first came, just after the war. I grew and changed but the trees had not. They stood tall and still then as they do today, bridging the past and the present. They provided some tangible proof of my existence, stuffing my doll dreams with reality.

I don't have any pictures of that time, but I carry some around in my imagination. They are like all old photos, yellowing, dog-eared and really only half remembered. Faded snapshots in a photo album unearthed from the back of a cupboard. Adults and children in quaintly dated clothes, quaint language, mannerisms and preoccupations quite beyond the understanding of my own children.

Those snapshots lie in an untidy heap strewn about the floor of my memory. Experiences and impressions don't come in neat and tidy bundles tied up with ribbon. It would be nice to have someone to go through them with; someone to share that toe-curling pleasure when some clue, a word, a name, a line of a song prompts a whole new avenue of recollection. Six years is most of one's childhood and no one has ever asked me what happened in those years. I didn't talk about it much because it was too hard to explain. It was as though when I went away I merely became invisible and didn't quite exist.

No one seemed to realise that things actually happened to me. This distanced me from people and it took me a long time to make that journey back. It was only when I had my own family and lived some of the experiences of other people that I felt I had properly come home. That is not to say that I enjoyed this distance. Being naturally rather friendly, it pained me and I tried very hard to overcome what I sensed to be my strangeness to other people.

So it is purely for my own entertainment I will sort and sift a frayed assortment of images into a kind of order that may fool me into believing I have illumined those twists and turns of childhood's shadowy paths.

As I look back and scan the pages in my album of recollections I look with an adult's eye at the perceptions of a child. I place an adult's construction upon the experiences and events that occurred long ago. Distance lends both a little enchantment and a little perspective to my view, it smooths the edges and trims the corners. My snapshots can be juggled around, placed beside each other or overlaid, they are inconsistent, changing their nature from opaque to transparent at a whim.

But is it true? Well all I can say is truth is sometimes what you want it to be. A pebble of childhood experience often goes unnoticed and soon forgotten at the time, but it drops to the bottom of the pond and makes up the silt of the grown-up mind. Perhaps changed in certain characteristics, but in nature essentially the same. Memories of memories intermingled with fresh news and visions interrupted in the long passage of time.

Some memories are so sharp and clear they're like needles. I stood beneath those trees and I saw snow lying heavy and ponderous on the branches as I had in the winter of 1947. I could almost touch it and cold settled around me as it had that year. I have never known cold as I did that winter. Standing quite still I am forced back inside that house.

The uneven sound of voices rising and falling trickles down the stairs and along the hallways, door handles turn and click shut. Footsteps pit-pat on stone pathways, while the wind hurly-burlys in the bushes and treetops. I catch a glimpse of the paper boy swinging up the drive and the wheels of his bike rasp on the gravel of the drive and he whistles the same tune. Five stones rattle on the wooden floor of the bay window in the schoolroom. Little stinging bites of sadness swell and bruise inside the eyelids, the throat and chest are furred by desolation.

Other episodes are buried more deeply. I have to search them out, screw up my eyes and wait for sudden recognition. I see a passage and can't tell where it leads, doors open into nowhere. Like Alice down the rabbit hole, familiar objects grow huge, then shrink and finally vanish altogether.

Sometimes I am small again and mingle with those unchanging children and then grow tall again and walk the dusty floors peering into desks and drawers. A visitor, a guest doing a tour of inspection, taking an inventory. Seeking what is hidden, prying into secrets that have no wish to be told.

Flickers of an earlier time, before I came to The Elms hover uncertainly about the edges of those serious trees. As they bend and part and lean upon the wind, the sky blooms huge and high, pale grey, stretching into forever, flowing out over the houses, the garden, the park; over the stream, over red setters scrambling for sticks and the trees gracefully posed in elegant arrangements.

At home in London's little streets of little houses there didn't seem to have been much sky. Only at night when the searchlights raked the dull blackness and the guns hammered away into the beams of straight white light, did the sky exist. Bombs fell from it and all kinds of noises spouted and died in the sky. The air raid warnings, the all clear sirens and that terrible whine that became a terrible silence; all these came from the sky. My father was up there too, somewhere high in the sky. This was a different sky. I no longer looked through windows criss-crossed with brown sticky paper, bordered by chintz, covered in lace, each with its own thick blackout blind.

The war was home, the only home I had ever known and after, the cold empty quiet chilled my childish soul. Now I had no home. The war didn't suddenly split our lives, it picked at them until they slowly unravelled and their original form could no longer be recognised. That empty silence crept upon me. Going to school was only a part of the gradual realisation that everything was different. It was when I came back for the holidays the house seemed strange and no longer home. The war had been full of people coming and going, full of urgency and significance. Even I had been taken out to celebrate V.E. day and V.J. day when the lights had come on in London, when it was all going to be so wonderful now that the war was over. But it wasn't, it was deadly dreary and the house was sad. A sadness that I swallowed down whole. My father had been killed and my grandfather had died in the same year. The same black clothes were worn for both funerals.

We were a house of women. My mother's dream of moving away from East London, she had so nearly achieved, but now she was back in the house she had grown up in. We didn't sleep under the table or under the stairs or in the shelter any more. No more sudden journey's in the night, when I would be taken from my bed and carried by torchlight to the bottom of the garden. No longer was I pushed to the pavement when the siren went in the street. There were no new faces around the breakfast table or people jostling each other to wash at the kitchen sink, while others squeezed behind them to put the kettle on for pots of tea. Even the conversation was different. No more talk of fire watching and the A.R.P. The tin hats had gathered dust on the hallstand and Uncle Charles the G.I. who seemed so huge he filled the whole door, had taken Auntie Elsie off to Arizona.

My mother's brother Eddie had married and moved to the north. Slowly the life had drained out of our existence, like a noisy train that had shunted into a siding and been forgotten. Now we were left with the rationing, the queues, the trips to the food office and enquiries about pension books. My grandmother had stopped wearing her dark blue serge trousers, my mother was always at work building a new structure to her world and to me the sorrow was impenetrable. Nanny's tutting disapproval of almost everything had hardened into ritualistic nagging that drove my mother further away from us.

The house had been shaken and cracked, the distemper had pattered from the ceiling and windows had blown in, but still it stood. Like the rest of the street it stood among the rubble of bomb sites around us. I too was left, a little remnant of the war, a strong-willed nosey five year old.

When my mother tried to salvage something of her broken dreams it was decided I should go away from London to boarding school in Surrey. I had already been to nursery for quite a long time and must have been a fairly sturdy child, for I was told that on one occasion, when I trotted in unexpectedly early, I casually announced 'the nursery got bombed today, Nanny'.

I am told I did not linger over my goodbyes at the big London station but left my mother without a backward glance when I set off on my long journey into the rest of my life. Truthfully I didn't really understand I would not be coming back to them that very night. But I was off, down to Sidmouth for the six weeks holiday before the start of the Autumn term. Gradually as the days passed it dawned upon me, I was here to stay.

At first the days spent playing on the sand were pleasant and there was a large rocking horse in the play room with which I was particularly entranced. I caught chicken pox, which I called 'poisonous spots', and I was isolated in a room rather like an attic. Then I knew for the first time I was a long way from home. Peering through the bars at the end of the bed during those long hours alone in that room I felt as though I was in a large box and someone had thrown away the key so no one would ever find me again. I have no idea how long I was there, but the loneliness and the terrible sense of isolation and rejection I have never forgotten. When I left that room I was not quite the same child that had gone in, a small kernel of real insight of what my life was to be had formed within me. My trust in human beings had been shaken. Never again would I wholeheartedly believe in anyone.

The Misses Meadmore

The Elms was one of those small private boarding schools that are dotted around the leafy edges of London. They are not at all as people imagine them to be. It is for this reason that I felt the urge to set down a few of my personal experiences of a 'private boarding school'. They are often considered to be places of wealth and privilege. Well, very expensive ones may be, but the small cheap private school is often peopled by children who have been plucked from their normal family life for one reason or another, find themselves in a totally strange environment and just have to make the best of it in any way they can. There is no Mum to run to, no shoulder to cry on and it doesn't take long to realise that you are on your own and that you have to fight your own battles. You keep your private sorrows to yourself and hold your head up with a dreadful inner pride, keep your own counsel and make your own judgements.

The school was run by three sisters who rejoiced in the name of Meadmore. The eldest I saw only a few times. She lived down in Sidmouth, which I now take to be the family home. It was here that I was first brought when I left London and apart from the 'attic room' and the rocking horse, I have only very hazy images of windows and floorboards. I stayed there for the six weeks of the school holidays, I think in order to acclimatize me to my forthcoming years at school. I do not recall being taken from Sidmouth to Surrey, but I must have been taken by train for the second time and deposited at The Elms with several other children. My one clear picture of the Sidmouth Miss Meadmore was of a large furry white mound of body topped by a pleasant cheerful ruddy face, leaning round a door and saying 'Goodbye'. The other Miss Meadmores did not communicate quite so readily with their charges, so this smiling open countenance stands out like a beacon in the memory of those years at The Elms.

The first Surrey Miss Meadmore had white hair that lay on her head like grubby white cotton wool held in a net. It didn't ever seem to move or change it's shape, gave no hint that it was composed of separate strands, but remained always in the same round mass stuck on her head. She was very fat, not a soft roly poly fatness nor an inviting plumpness. Her fat was lard-hard and solid. When she walked her legs did not appear to bend at the knees. She would stomp on lumpen feet along the wooden floor and each step sounded like a mallet driving in a stake. The sound of those relentless footsteps echoed around the house. For us children it was like an early warning system. We froze in attitudes of obedience at the first blow. Of course we made fun of her behind her back, as we viewed those buttresses of legs carrying the great bulk of buttocks heaving from side to side down the passageway. This Miss Meadmore greeted parents and children as they arrived, beckoning and inviting visitors into the 'lounge'. Lowering her great bottom sideways into a large and comfortable armchair she would compose her features into an imitation of a smile. A reasonably good imitation because parents were taken in by it certainly and also children, at least, at first. However after that first brief encounter we were never graced by this smile again.

Miss Meadmore was a person of great and terrible rage. Her face would swell up like a purple Victoria plum, in danger of bursting at any time. This furnace of rage could sweep down upon you suddenly and unpredictably. You realised that in some particular way you had erred, but Miss Meadmore didn't waste time on questions and explanations. That great hand like a shovel, that massive forearm, delivered hearty wallops in all directions and you bounced about like marbles under the impact. Now I realise that the really naughty things we did went unpunished because of course she never knew about them. We were only punished for acts we did not consider especially dreadful. We would never have been deliberately naughty anywhere near her, being all too well aware of the purple wrath we would bring down upon our heads. I lied hugely all the time and skulked at the back of the crowd whenever possible, trying to make myself even smaller than I was.

Her favourite word was 'thrashing'.

"You'll get a good thrashing".

These words would be enunciated clearly and with relish through her rigid teeth and straight mouth. We were afraid of her, but this did not seem to affect us. Once outside her appalling presence, an awful resourcefulness grew in us. We remained bloody but unbowed. It was a point of honour not to cry when one of these 'thrashings' with a slipper or a hairbrush was administered.

"Did you cry?" was the first question that was asked when any one of us returned, our flesh red and burning from the encounter. Of course we did cry and when we cried, which we all did into our pillows, into the secret darkness of the night, it was silently and alone. We did not look to each other for comfort.

Apart from presiding over the 'lounge' and disseminating false bonhommie to adults, Miss Meadmore's main activities seemed to revolve around the kitchen. Not only did she rule us children with her great and terrible rage, she also had two young maids in her power. They were never the same two young maids. One pair was particularly lively and spoke to us and told us jokes as if we were real people. They did not stay long.

Meals were heralded by the ringing of the gong. A marvellous reverberating noise that rolled around every crevice of the house. Wherever you were, that glorious throbbing boom could penetrate any door however far away. Miss Meadmore was the queen of the dinner table. Large dishes and tureens would be brought in and put on a table near the door, little curls of steam played over heaps of potatoes and greens. She would sit behind the table wielding large ladles and serving spoons like sceptres. A face of harsh unremitting severity dishing up delicious dinners of roast beef, Yorkshire pudding, gravy and greens, and boiled potatoes. I loved the dinners, but I wasn't so keen on the afters. I especially disliked pink blancmange and tapioca that seemed to be served horribly often. On one occasion I refused to eat my tapioca. I just sat there quite mute.

"Very well, you will sit there until you do eat it." I was commanded inevitably.

But I didn't eat it. I just went on sitting there. I don't know how I had the courage to be so defiant, it must have been brute stupidity. Or perhaps I thought the 'thrashing' was a lesser evil than the tapioca. Eventually the maids took pity on me and sneaked it out of the room and threw it away when no one was looking.

The dining room was a pleasant room with French windows overlooking a flight of stone steps leading down to the garden. The room was light and airy with several long tables arranged around it, with benches to sit on. Because Miss Meadmore sat by the door, it was possible to escape her ferocious stare and enjoy your food in relative peace. Sometimes there were two other teachers and even though I was so young I remember feeling sorry for them and being dimly aware that they were trapped in the Meadmore's web of tyranny more tightly than we children. There were all kinds of little bolt holes, schemes, games and escape routes for us. Also we could hide and melt into a raggle taggle collection of children. The few lone teachers had no cover at all, they were mercilessly exposed. Pathetic middle aged spinsters clinging to a semblance of life by the skin of their teeth, keeping themselves alive as best they could. The Meadmores held them in contempt and made no secret of the fact. The first Miss Meadmore would occasionally address a few words to them in her odd barking tone accompanied by her grim smile. Her face when not twisted by fury, was normally bright pink as if she had come to rest after great exertion. Maybe she had, perhaps that's why her words were delivered in such sharp bursts.

Anyway Miss Metcalfe and Miss Polsue (for these were their names) replied deferentially and never at length, not seeming to wish to prolong any conversation. Miss Meadmore would stomp back to the kitchen and robustly hurl aside anyone who happened to be in her path. If she came upon a group of us unexpectedly in front of her, with arms flailing in all directions, she would hack her way through us like Livingstone in the jungle. Slower or weaker members often found themselves on the floor after one of these vigorous flurries. You learned to skip out of the way pretty nippily. If we were between maids, as we frequently were, it was our job to help fetch and carry plates and cutlery. You went in fear and trembling of being thrown to the ground while carrying a pile of china, so we would wait for each other and travel in convoy; at least we would all hit the deck together.

Throughout those six years, although children left and others replaced them, we were all deeply united, almost unconsciously, against the Meadmores.

Our whole lives were punctuated by these great charges down the passage to the kitchen. The kitchen was two rooms, both rather crowded and disorganised. Lovely smells wafted out of there, but we never went in when food was actually being prepared. We were only permitted to see the aftermath. There was an enormous fridge with double doors like a white wardrobe that rattled and clattered. We occasionally climbed in when no one was looking just to find out what it was like inside. What made it so inviting was the bright light, which probably saved our skins, for it was no fun to close the doors tightly and be in the dark.

Some guardian angel must have been very busy saving us from ourselves as we darted from one misadventure to another. Miss Meadmore, for all her ferocity, never seriously quelled the spirits of her charges and for most of the time was blissfully unaware of our energetic private lives. Presumably she was in charge of the administration of the school and its day-to-day running, for she never took any lessons— thank heaven. Her domain, her natural habitat, was the lounge and we were only permitted into this inner sanctum on very rare occasions with our parents. The 'lounge' was the pleasantest room in the house, for it had carpet on the floor, with a large brightly coloured pattern with lots of blue and it was deep and soft to the tread. There were huge chintz covered armchairs and a settee and curtains that stretched from floor to ceiling; something I'd never seen before. It was so different from everywhere else to be almost in another house. No one ever wanted to go in that beautiful room with its soft lights from several table lamps and its pretty colours and comfortable fabrics. Many a 'thrashing' was executed in that delightful room before that white sculptured marble fireplace.

In the evening Miss Meadmore took off her voluminous charlady's overall and replaced her somewhat skimpy floral dress, that rose up high over her hips, for another almost identical skimpy floral dress. Her swollen thighs and calves separated by ridged flesh behind her knees pounded into the 'lounge' and she disappeared behind the closed door. From the crack under the door a yellow beam splayed across the hall floor. Pools of light and gentle shadows settled on the staircase and wooden boards, softening the contours of the house. It was night and for all creatures that don't like the light, now was the time for the revels to begin.

If you went up the staircase, with its carved polished rail, and stood on the mezzanine and looked up, you could see the balustrade of the long landing above. It was always dark as a cave. Several doors led onto it, they were always kept closed. From the furthest door like the innermost recess of a Pharoah's tomb would emerge a dim form. It shambled from that uttermost door appearing at first glance to be a large pile of dirty washing heaped upon the floor. A slight shuffling scuffing noise could be discerned and the heap moved with great difficulty into the first pat of greyish light on the landing, until this curious pile revealed itself to be the other Miss Meadmore. Holding tightly to the rail of the balustrade she would stand surveying the staircase. As often as possible she would direct her daily operations from this vantage point, delaying for as long as possible the immense task of actually descending the stairs. A moment, as long awaited as the second coming, on some days.

At weekends this Miss Meadmore never got beyond this point. Her tasks for the day being completed, she would shamble back into her lair and would not be seen again until the following day. Only the sight of trays of food being delivered and collected gave any hint of her presence. These trays would be placed on a table outside her room, visible proof that she did eat, for she was never seen in the dining room with the rest of us. Hers must have been quite a large room because it was over the schoolroom in the front of the house. No one had ever seen inside this capacious cell and only very rarely had anyone even observed the door a tiny crack open. It was as though she had some miraculous power to move through the wall. This Miss Meadmore was in charge of the schoolroom. After breakfast, as we cleared away our porage bowls (which I also loved) she would appear as usual at the top of the stairs.

Her strong muscular fingers would be planted firmly around the bannister rail and she would manoeuvre her weight with great care onto one leg. Her other leg would be lowered to meet the first. In this way she would heavily descend the stairs one step at a time. When she reached the small mezzanine landing where the stair turned around she would pause. Here she would put two hands on the rail and shuffle on soft shoes round the bend in readiness to attempt the last flight of steps. The bannisters groaned and squeaked under her immense weight and the wooden stairs sagged wearily. At the bottom we children were all clustered respectfully around, hovering in anxious anticipation for the final descent to the floor. It wasn't long before a stick became a part of her normal accoutrements. She was permanently bent forward with one hand on her stick and the other on any handy wall or piece of furniture. In this position it would seem as if her head grew from her great haunches, as she leaned her neck up and back, tortoise fashion.

Because of the great physical incapacity and her collection of shroud-like garments, she seemed to be a lot older than the first Miss Meadmore. However this was not borne out by her head. Her hair, though straggly, was still a definite nut brown, set in iron waves. A pair of very alert round brown eyes came as a great surprise from that huge shapeless mound of body. A mind of sharp intelligence and wit dominated our basic education.

She was of course a very severe schoolmistress, very much of the breed of her generation, but she did not radiate an aura of hostility like her sister. She was capable of genuine amusement, even merriment and would laugh quite freely with staff and children if anything caught her fancy. True she would also laugh at you with uncomfortable frequency and she sharpened her wits on your ignorance and discomforture. This lighter side of her nature did not extend as far as actual kindness, but she exercised a certain rigorous justice in her dealings with us children. She was more the professional teacher who conceded merit where it was deserved and meted out punishment in a similarly detached manner. Her relationship with us was characterised by a distance of emotional separateness. One word from the second Miss Meadmore could make you squirm at fifty paces. We didn't really like her, but we didn't really hate her either. The small flame of white hot hatred in all our wicked little hearts was reserved exclusively for the first Miss Meadmore. If we had ever run amok I think we would cheerfully have hacked her to pieces.

Once the second Miss Meadmore was finally settled behind her large desk she still managed to overflow around the sides. Her feet were so splayed that if you were called to the desk, the closest you could stand was still a few feet away from her. A large black ebony ruler reposed on the front of the desk and any misdemeanour was dealt with swiftly. Miss Meadmore was considerably more powerful sitting down than standing up and she would deliver the required number of wacks upon the outstretched hand of the miscreant with mechanical precision. Effortlessly and with practised ease Miss Meadmore would perform this task. Because of the peculiar distance involved, the end of the ruler would come down on the centre of the palm like the point of a knife. Upon the command 'sit down' the unfortunate wretch would return to its seat and sit on its hand for a while. It did not take long for everyone to understand that if you sat still and did as you were told you were quite safe from the ebony ruler.

Once Miss Meadmore was finally esconced on her chair behind the desk, she remained grounded to her spot, the sprawling trunk of a felled oak. The drapery of all those layers of clothes twisted about like aerial roots on the floor. Only her neck would turn and crane around— even behind her. The shining brown eyes swept every corner of the room. They swept above our heads, but never penetrated the tucks and folds of our minds.

She set us our tasks and we did what was asked of us. Never once were we troubled by any enquiry into the content of our thoughts. In the strictly organised quiet of the classroom the most exciting thing to do was think. I have no idea how much I learned of my lessons, but I definitely learned how to think. Young as I was the realisation of the immense power of one's private thoughts was strongly formed. When my turn came to face judgement, my already strong will was flexed and strengthened by the trial. 'You can make me do what you want, but you cannot get inside my mind', was the phrase I would hug tightly into myself. I became very choosy about what I would accept from adults and what I would not. It took a long time for me to realise that people are influenced by stealth, and what is charming pleasant and delightful is not always good.

Miss Meadmore not only resided over our morning lessons but also the playroom. Painfully she waddled down the hall, leaning heavily on a chair rail, with her skirts dipping around her ankles. She would pause at the door of the playroom and gesture for the table to be cleared and her chair put in its usual place. Her demeanour was less severe in the evening. She had come to preside over the feeding and bedding down of the cats.

The Elms was not only a refuge of refugees but also a home for cats. At various times thirty or more cats were in residence at the school and there was no doubt whatsoever that the cats were held in far higher esteem by the Meadmores than the children, teachers, or other staff. Everything was provided for their comfort and well being, even to the extent that the children were really only suffered in the playroom— it was truthfully the cat's boudoir. These were the real children of the second Miss Meadmore and she was rarely seen without one of them as an appendage to her voluminous person. Even in the classroom she usually had one draped across her bosom.

Once she was enthroned on her special chair behind the long wooden table, she would survey the mound of soft raw meat that was placed before her. With a butcher's skill she sliced through the flesh and sinews with a very sharp wicked-looking knife. She cut and sliced deftly until the meat was reduced to small chunks. Her fingers squeezed around these, sunk deeply into the flesh and with infinite precision, she would dice them into tiny pieces. Calling the cats by name she lobbed handfuls of these tiny pieces of meat at their feet. If any one of them showed signs of greed or unruly grabbing, she tapped their noses with her foot and sent them shying away.

The whole operation was quite lengthy and Miss Meadmore took her time ensuring that no cat went unfed. There must have been nearly thirty cats to feed every night and Miss Meadmore enjoyed a little entertainment while she busied herself with the carving and slicing. One or more of us might be called upon to stand under the mantel shelf by the stove and sing 'Run Rabbit Run' or 'Put Another Nickel In'

The dark winter evenings could be quite convivial when Miss Meadmore was feeling particularly jolly. Even the first Miss Meadmore might look in and pleasantries were exchanged between the two women. The conversation flowed over our heads, but the atmosphere was pleasant. Under the harsh glare of the naked light bulbs that mercilessly showed up the bareness of the playroom with its untreated floorboards and curtainless windows, there was a sensation of warmth and comfort.

When the cats had to be gathered in our help was always enlisted, to call in the garden and bang tin plates until the last was ushered into the house. Occasionally the odd renegade, that had strayed too far could not be accounted for and Miss Meadmore made a superhuman effort to struggle to the French windows to call him herself.

After the ritual feeding of the cats, we were slowly edged out of the playroom. Cats, bits of meat, saucers of milk, boxes were all over the place. Eventually their boxes were strewn over the whole room. Their invasion was complete when there was barely enough space for us to stand on the floor. The cats swaggered about with their tails in the air, sniffing and snooty as they made their choice of resting place. Some ignored the boxes, preferring the window ledge or the top of a cupboard, where they glowered down at us.

Now we were the unwelcome intruders in their private suite where they stretched themselves and washed themselves and each other. Ominous scratching of sharp talons on bare wood seemed designed to hasten our departure.

Only the second Miss Meadmore was to be tolerated and she remained like Britannia ruling her sea of cats. They would climb all over her and often come to rest upon her vast pillow of chest. By this time we had our backs to the door and our last vision of the second Miss Meadmore was of a heaving furry mound.

All the boys trundled upstairs, for they slept in the main house and the girls tripped and skipped out into the garden and along the pathway to the 'other house'. Both Miss Meadmores were left to their respective dens and matron busied herself with the smaller boys.

We little girls had one whole enormous house all to ourselves.

The 'Other House'

The school was not really a school at all, it was two big houses that stood side by side with a sizeable gap between them. I imagine they had once been private houses built for a wealthy family. The garden at the back and the long curve of the sweeping drive in the front gave no hint they had ever been separated. Facing the main road was a low wooden fence which was one continuous line with a gate at either end. All activity revolved around the first house which stood at the corner of another road leading from the main arterial road. Postmen, tradesmen, visitors all tramped up and down the path to the big door at the top of the stone steps of the first house. It was a very imposing entrance way. But I did not enjoy the grandeur of it, being too overcome by its size and the darkness of the hall that lay behind the great door. The children did not use the front door in their daily comings and goings, instead we tripped in and out of the more comfortable back door.

The 'other house' appeared overlooked and sheepish like a poor relation its grander neighbour was trying to ignore. It was almost completely hidden by thick tangled dusty dark ivy. The stems were strong and woody as though the house itself was a growing living tree. One day a handsome prince was to hack his way through with his sword and wake us with a kiss. This was our castle, our ivory tower. We were at once prisoners and kings in our kingdom. What we did there, what we talked about, what we plotted and planned and played— our cruelties, squabbles and acts of childish villany— were never mentioned at any other time. The conspiracy of childhood was absolute. This was not a deliberate act or an intentional desire for secrecy. We were like the fairies at the bottom of the garden, separate and uniquely different creatures from any adult who assumed they had charge over us.

Inside, the house was quite different from the first house. It was huge and empty as if everyone had gone away or died suddenly. When you stepped inside from a small back door and walked down a short passageway, you came into what seemed like the great hall of a deserted palace. A patterned mosaic floor of stone radiated from the knewel post at the bottom of the stairs, which was the focal point of the hall. The staircase wound gently down to the floor and flared where the bannister rail ended in a tight little wooden spiral kept polished and shiny by all the soft tummies that slid down it. It was delicious to trace your finger round and round the snaky coils in the wood. Above you the ceiling was so high it went on forever and you never noticed it at all. The smallest sound rolled round and round the vast emptiness of this vast amphitheatre of the house. An awareness of the sheer theatricality of it all bit deeply into us for we played at queens and princesses and Marlene Dietrich, majestically descending the stairs. With our dressing gowns tied around our waists to form flowing skirts, we regally surveyed admiring courtiers below. Although none of us possessed anything more than the contents of one small drawer of socks and underclothes, we owned this mansion, this palace, this castle, this stately home. Outside, the gardens, orchard, lily pond, the park across the road, were all our lands and our estates.

Several doors led from this central hall into sad silent rooms with tall staring vacant windows. A cold anonymous dull light fell upon the rooms, making them look flat and uninteresting. Curiosity drove us to peep into them all, but once we had seen them we never went into them again. They were like discarded old boots and shoes no one had any use for any more. Grandeur we could enjoy and take our part in, secret places and forbidden territory we annexed and raucously pillaged. But these rejected rooms touched a raw nerve. We did not wish to be associated in any way with what was rejected, démodé, surplus to requirements. You could catch a whiff in the air at any time of an unspoken sneaking suspicion that we were like those rooms that no one had any use for. It hung around and clung to us like stale smoke. Even the ghosts had deserted the house. The only suggestion of other human life was a notice saying 'Conservative Committee Rooms'.

We waited for someone to hold a meeting, but no one ever came. The heavy front door stood in darkness, permanently bolted. Late in the afternoon pale sunlight would trickle down the stairs washing over the patterned floor from a high window above. Odd nooks and crannies would be briefly illumined, it was a sigh before sunset when the shadows raised themselves from their great burden and stretched and eased their bones before the night. Discomforted by the sudden exposure, the dusty corners would settle back into obscurity with relief as the sun slid behind the chimney pot of the first house.

Neglect had become accustomed and cozy; faded walls and skirting boards no longer welcomed any attention. Like the spiders, the field mice and house martins, we scampered about the house turning to our use what cracks and corners took our fancy. Rolling over each other, under beds, careering from bedroom to bedroom pushing and shoving. Our short cries, shrieks and squeals sprayed into the air bouncing off the high ceilings. Each sound cannoning into the next. This trilling mushroomed into one long balloon of noise, pressing on the walls of the house with such force you felt the bricks might crack. Apparently, only if like Jericho, the walls had come tumbling down, would anyone have come to enquire into our activities. Very occasionally some ancient instinct warned us of matron's approach along the path outside. Momentarily our ears stood up, then in a twinkling we were all back in our beds and under the covers.

The two houses stood together, side by side, but in reality they were opposite poles of our universe. When I was in the presence of either of the Meadmores in the first house, I always felt dull, drab and lumpish with nothing to commend me. I felt spectacularly lacking in any cleverness or talents but as soon as we entered the 'other house' that leaden feeling evaporated. Our spirits and our bodies became light. Tongues loosened, animation spread among us bright and sparky, a fever of imagination tossed us into one hectic game after another.

Our dormitories were upstairs and all the rooms led off a very wide L shaped landing. There were about five or six beds in my room. There was a fireplace with a narrow mantelpiece, a rickety chest of drawers and that was about all. The windows had no curtains and seemed enormous. They dominated the room and appeared to stretch from wall to wall and floor to ceiling. Yet we used to sit on the low sills which were more comfortable than the beds. These had iron bars along the sides of the sagging bedsprings. If you sat down your bottom plummetted and your legs sprang up to meet your nose. Once trapped in this position, like being in a collapsed deckchair, you had to summon assistance to be hauled up again. Here in the dormitory we struggled to grow up and profound discussions took place about periods, hair styles, and the best way to arrange our drawers. I don't know whether we behaved like children would in a family, but it didn't feel the same. Having this great house all to ourselves for such long hours we often played at being grown-ups. One little girl with long brown curling hair, shiny bright eyes and rosebud mouth was always offering us imaginary cigarettes and generously inviting us to have another drink. "Oh, darling, do have a Martini". This phrase was accompanied by graceful gestures of her hands and puckering of the lips as she blew pretend smoke into the air. I was most impressed and practised earnestly, until under her tutelage we seriously rivalled Bette Davis and Joan Crawford.

My own experience of grown-ups was more to do with blackleading the kitchen range and stirring the washing in a steaming copper. This novel behaviour introduced a whole new dimension into my life. Nina (I think that was her name) pulled off her vests and socks with a similar waving kind of nonchalance. All her movements were slow and languorous and utterly entrancing. Alas, however much I copied her, I ended up looking as if I were sending semaphore messages to the fleet. I pined for curly hair and spent hours tying it up in rags (a method I had read about in books). Perfectly good handkerchiefs ended up in shreds because of this preoccupation.

I emerged with a horrible frizz and a nasty sharp telling off for my pains, which added to my misery. Then the boys all jeered at me, but I wasn't put off. I was going to be glamourous or die in the attempt. The more they told me I was a vain and wicked girl, the more determined I became. They washed our hair in black soap and I was convinced it contained sinister properties to make your hair straight to keep you ugly.

In the holidays I exasperated my mother and drove my grandmother to nervous hysteria by my insistence on always wearing hair ribbons to match my clothes of which there were only a few that I actually liked. I absolutely hated the bulgy vests and knickers I was made to wear, especially knickers. The great knicker war lasted for about ten years.

Nina was unique in her gracefulness. The rest of us ranged from dimpled plumpness to wiry thinness. I came somewhere in the middle having a large rib cage, solid muscular legs and a protruding tummy that finally went down like a balloon when I was about twelve. Years of ballet lessons eventually trained my shape to mask its natural athleticism.

We were all in awe of Valerie, because Valerie had an almost properly grown bosom. We would inspect ourselves regularly anxiously waiting for the moment when ours would begin to grow. I had a very long wait, even then the results were disappointing.

We were a fairly cosmopolitan bunch. There were Greeks, Cypriots, Poles, German Jews, Irish, as well as English children from other parts of the country. Fragments of conversation that seep back make me now realise it was the war that had thrown us all up on the same beach.

Home was somewhere else and was never a burning topic of conversation, but the odd detail or incident would crop up that shed some light on our shadowy backgrounds. Two rather sad little waifs stayed for a time and it was rumoured their parents had died in Belsen.

The 'other house' was always full of intrigue and secret revenges on the Meadmores would be examined with relish, only to be abandoned the next day when confronted with the reality. The older children voiced their resentment more strongly than the young ones. We would listen delightedly to the hot indignation in their voices as they passionately declared what they would do and say when the big moment came. I especially enjoyed Denise's perorations and pleaded to be allowed to take part in the plotting when they tried to push me away because I was too young. She was a big girl and always especially vituperative. I had great hopes of Denise to lead us to some ultimate salvation. No one ever did anything. We fought a rear guard action instead with Denise organising all kinds of other subversion from the headquarters of the 'other house'.

Mavis, Allanha, Jill, June, Anna, some names I can even put a face to, while other faces remain nameless. I can see each one separately in a short choreographed sequence that is repeated over and over again in my mind's eye.

Mavis stands transfixed, in paralysed stillness, while we giggle around her and take things out of her hand. We'd never heard of 'petit mal'. All we knew was that Mavis, in full flood of earnest indignation, would suddenly stop dead and go into what we called 'one of her trances', her large head and heavy features holding the same unwavering expression. After a few seconds of standing 'en attitude', often with her hands outstretched before her like a wax work figure, she would resume her outburst quite unaware she had momentarily dropped out of this life.

Anna forever pelts down a flight of stone steps after me, hot footing it to the bushes. "I'll bash you Windy Pitt"...never realising those words would be petrified in my memory.

Allanha is framed by the brightness of the window and her face is in shadow. She is a saintly silhouette quietly reading, her long dark hair falling softly to her shoulders. Her dress is dark and sombre, a little Irish Bernadette.

June, salmon pink with ginger hair. June Parry from an island...Canvey, Hayling...Something Island, she must have been a special friend of mine. She appears tiny, but more clearly defined, as in a camera obscura, she accompanies me on many escapades.

Jill has a whole act, a complete scenario all to herself. They are now children from the never never land, children who didn't grow up.

Gooseberries

Two's company and threes a crowd. We were company for each other, but always in a crowd. Perhaps special friendships were formed, but I was never aware of them. I was only conscious of being part of a crowd, the faces changed from time to time, but mostly we did things together. In the early years I often felt pangs of exclusion, but once I was thoroughly adapted to my situation a manipulative faculty began to emerge in my nature. Loneliness is to be forever on the outside looking in, waiting to be invited to join the party. Twin buds slowly formed, one to be content with one's own company and the other was the capacity to instigate. I quickly learned how to grasp any opportunity that came my way to control matters.

Being literally at the mercy of the merciless, which could on occasions be other children as well as adults, the unrealised instincts of self preservation became honed and refined. Considerably more so in much later life, but the spade work was done at The Elms. A pattern of emotional and mental resourcefulness had been laid down and in the times of tribulation all lives contain, I could usually wriggle out of them reasonably unscathed.

Daylight hours in the 'other house' contrasted sharply with the night. Squealing, pelting, romping, play acting subsided from bright flames to glowing embers. As night settled around us we felt the whispers of the humming world beyond, calling us through the dark glass panes. The black trees' branches swayed, the grass and the bushes shivered with some secret excitement. Our small bodies caught the mood and quivered at the mystery surrounding us. Some irresistible current tugged at our footsteps. We followed in a mixture of joy and terror. It was a curious rite that we must all go through and if we failed we would remain forever weak and lesser beings. The supreme test of our courage and future strength of character was to hitch up our nightdresses and tiptoe barefoot down the stairs and out of the house into the silent night.

At the back of the 'other house' was a greenhouse set against the wall of the house. In front was a triangular piece of lawn with a long fence, which ran along the longest side of the triangle. Once outside the house, we would hold our breath and creep along the path full of suppressed giggles, past the greenhouse to the furthest edge of the fence. Squeezing ourselves behind the bushes and flattened against the fence, where the slightest sharp movement made the twigs snap and crackle, we inched our way along, our hearts nearly bursting in our chests, until the straight fence that bordered the main garden was ahead of us. Leaving the haven of the brush we scurried across a bright patch of moonlit grass, then, past the familiar smell of the compost heap, we ducked into the orchard. The trees rose up above us huge and laden, the tips of their branches touching and lacing in the slight summer breeze.

We sneaked along bent low, to the gooseberry bushes. Our greedy little fingers probed and plucked among the prickles and protective leaves, unheeding of the jagged tears in our soft skins. Spreading our skirts like bags we filled them with small, shiny, hard green gooseberries. Long trails of light from the main house gazed unwinkingly into the night. Oozing over the rose bushes, filtering through the trellis and dying on the bald patch on the playground. A vacant light quite blind to the little band industriously stripping the bushes in the deepest reaches of the orchard.

When our skirts were so bulging with gooseberries that they kept trickling out of the side however tightly we tugged the sides together, we decided we had enough. Bent double, we staggered along with our booty. The journey back to the bedroom had none of the frisky excitement of the outgoing trip. We bumped into each other and stubbed our toes on every stone. We had to risk the open ground and in our haste and clumsiness we dropped most of what we had gathered. We panted like dogs and our hands became sticky with sweat so the soggy cotton of our nightdresses was heavy and hard to hold. There were no more giggles, or even a smile, the effort to get back to the house undetected, took all our concentration. When we finally heaved ourselves into the sanctuary of our beds absolute jubilation overcame us. The enormity of what we had done swelled our hearts with wicked pride.

I don't remember who actually suggested this particular expedition but Denise's broad back filled my vision for much of the time. Hissed instructions and explosive noises emanated from just above her shoulder during most of the foray. I was usually an enthusiastic team member and her mantle of authority was not passed to me until later when she left.

On one particular night we sat cross-legged in our beds and dutifully crunched our way through a fair quantity of hard unripe gooseberries until we couldn't look another in the face. The eating was a long way second in importance to the getting. Greed was the spur for the expedition but it was soon supplanted by the thrill and excitement of adventure. We finally fell asleep among the debris of prickly, hairy, half-eaten remains, swilling about in our bedclothes. But there was a price to be paid for so great and glorious an episode.

The next day we all looked as green as the gooseberries and felt worse.

This had to be endured in stoic silence, no one daring to admit to the gut-wrenching pain that filled our whole bodies. After that, gooseberry picking was definitely out and we set our minds to other less painful excursions. The full price of retribution was yet to be paid and it was from me it would be exacted on another occasion.

If anyone had any money, which was very rare, we actually left the house and gardens altogether. After we were undressed and ready for bed, three of us got up and dressed again. With practised stealth we stole out of the house as usual, but this time we went right out of the gate to the main road. Like Olympic athletes we sprinted down the road to the chip shop in Carshalton.

"Three pennyworth of chips, please", we puffed and squeaked to the man behind the counter.

After carefully wrapping them up in our berets we pelted back to the house. Delicious floppy, luke warm chips filled six eager mouths when we shared them out with the others on our return.

Although these trips required great daring, in some way they were less satisfying than others, when we remained closer to the house. They took your breath away, but the prospect of actually being caught out in the street was so awful that it robbed you of the pleasure of the expedition. The bright lights of the shop and the ordinariness of the people engaged in familiar activities was not sufficient to feed our imagination. We craved mystery, darkness and secrecy. We wanted to be swallowed up in black holes, to be racked by waves and tremors of excitement; for our blood to turn to water and our spines to freeze.

It turned out that the very thing was right under our

noses— or our feet to be exact. One afternoon, when we were skulking through the undergrowth in the wilderness between the houses, one of the boys suddenly plopped out of sight like a rabbit down a hole. Seconds later he emerged, filthy and filled with delight. He had been pushing himself along through the long grass on his bottom, when he thought he had reached the wall of the house. He lifted his hands from the ground and leant forward to stand up, when his feet went straight through a tiny opening in the bricks that led right under the house. We all clustered around and peered into the opening, that was just large enough for a child to creep through. There was nothing to be seen but thick draperies of cobwebs. A dank earthy smell assailed our nostrils. We just stood there staring down into a cavernous nothingness when slowly, very slowly it dawned on us. Secret passages!

The words ripped through us like a forest fire. This was 'such stuff as dreams are made of', this was what boarding school was all about. We knew because we'd read about it. Hadn't we been faithful to generations of 'boarders' by following the great tradition laid down in all the books? This was what our moonlight expeditions had all been about. And now the final achievement, the ultimate endorsement of our existence. Secret passages! We could hardly contain ourselves. Immense visions rose before us of lost treasure, trap doors, panels with knots to be pressed, that would swing open and reveal...what? Oh, the mind pinged open wide, wide as an apple split into two by an arrow. This great discovery was rivalled only by the finding of the tomb of Tutankhamoun.

No one was to breathe a word and absolutely nothing was to be done until a comprehensive plan of campaign had been organised. It was far too momentous to rush into without extracting every ounce of sensation from it.

We had one major problem— the boys. Nearly all our nocturnal wanderings had been all female affairs entirely due to circumstance. No one objected to the boys, generally we quite liked having them around, but could they be trusted? They weren't the veterans we were. Could they keep a secret? Could they take the risk? Sleeping in the main house so close to the Meadmores presented an enormous and unnecessary obstacle, if they were to come with us.

Because we had no idea what they got up to in their private moments at bedtime, we had no idea how they would react. They were our daytime playmates and companions in arms against the Meadmores, but they were rather mild little boys who sulked more than we did when they got into trouble. All this agitation that the discovery had provoked left them slightly bewildered.

Muttering broke out and dissension about 'bossy girls' and 'who found it anyway?'

Followed by taunts of retaliation 'We'll go on our own so there!'

'And we'll tell on you mmmer!'

Division in the ranks produced a stalemate and left us undecided for some time as to the best course of action. Several of the girls were of the opinion that if we left it, the boys might forget and we could quietly investigate the 'great find' on our own in peace. A few thought that it might be too frightening and we could get lost.

The great debate continued in the playroom, in the cloakroom, outside the boys' toilets, behind the shed, in the playground. Practical June suggested that the boys might have useful items like matches, torches or they may even be able to get hold of some candles. This proved to be true and that settled it. They had shown themselves to be worthy of inclusion and had displayed an unsuspected resourcefulness. Now we would just have to wait and sniff out the best opportunity.

Inevitably fate took a hand. The only adult who might possibly be about after bedtime was Matron, who was Irish. Well, it just so happened that she was called away to Ireland at a most opportune moment. We were left in the hands of poor Miss Metcalfe who was anxious to slip away into her little room and listen to the radio. She was not going to linger in the bathroom, sort towels and sheets in the linen cupboard, or hover over the little ones once they were asleep.

It was nearly the end of the summer term, a certain relaxation had settled upon our enclosed community, the evenings were warm and friendly. Denise was leaving and she was full-blown with all the recklessness of her imminent liberation. She fizzed with energy as she organised her last campaign. The heaven-sent opportunity of Miss Metcalfe being in charge at bed time meant that we would, without a qualm, abuse her more kindly spirit. So, like the villains we were, we 'smiled and smiled again' and charmed her with our eagerness to help and see the little ones into bed. Lying winningly, we assured her that they were safely gathered in and the older boys always went first to the toilet downstairs and then put themselves to bed. Soothing her with our air of confidence we bade her goodnight and went downstairs. The boys were skulking below the stairs, kneeling on the benches outside the downstairs cloakroom. One bright brown eye kept watch peering out between the bannisters. When we reached the bottom step, they silently fell in with us and the little party passed through the dim long shadowed dining room and out into the garden.

Once on our own ground, we relaxed, sweet ingenuous smiles were replaced by harsher grins and we bared our teeth in glee. The boys emptied their pockets— it was quite a little haul they had amassed. A bent penknife, several candles, matches, razor blades, a couple of torches, a piece of chalk; these were the useful items. The screwed up 'horror comic' the five stones, marbles, bits of balsa wood, chewed pencils were statutory and so of little interest.

Some private foraging in the kitchen must have taken place without our knowledge, because grubby hairy slices of bread, bits of woody cheese and a kitchen knife finally emerged from the depths of a blazer pocket.

Only one of the torches worked and even that was yellow dim, so the candles were evenly distributed among us. There were about ten of us, a large party for a nocturnal ramble. In single file we tiptoed back downstairs and out into the garden, pausing at the back door to check for any sign of unusual movement. All was calm and commonplace, only the moths and gnats twitched in the lights from the playroom. John went first on his own, because he'd found the hole in the first place.

He vanished into the undergrowth. A few seconds later his head bobbed up again.

"It's here".

His strangled whisper was accompanied by frantic hand signals for us to join him. Moving awkwardly, two at a time, we scuttled across to where he was.

"Let's light the candles."

"No, not yet, someone might see."

"We can't see where we're going."

Excited muffled bickering continued, until someone, in a burst of impatience mingled with the fear of discovery if we hung around for much longer, imbued them with a sort of hopeless daring.

"Oh, I'll go down the hole first with a candle and hold it up for you to light".

Heroically they slithered into the hole and touched soft earth sooner than they expected. "It's ever so dark, quick light the candle. Several matches spilled onto the floor in our eagerness to obey. At last the candle sprang to life and we all breathed again. The person in the hole scratched around for our lost matches for what seemed like an age. We jostled and squashed each other to peer down into the hole. One at a time we crawled through the tiny opening. As more of us joined each other in the dark chamber below, so more candles were lit, until a surprising amount of light circled around. We stared fearfully about us, the ceiling was quite low, we could touch it with our hands. It was like a cellar and smelled overpoweringly earthy. There was absolutely nothing there but four brick walls and a floor of soft brown earth.

The opposite wall had a hole in it. We slowly moved towards it like a religious procession, our lighted candles held reverently, still and straight. A curious silence fell upon the little group. Our midnight adventure had changed its character entirely, it had become something closer to a pilgrimage. No one said a word, each of us seemed wrapt by the mysteriously tomb-like atmosphere. We were some secret society driven underground to meet unseen. We had come like the early Christians, stealthily creeping through the catacombs.

The hole in the wall was incredibly small, one at a time we heaved and pushed each other through, grazing our hands and legs on the rough bricks. The next chamber had an even lower ceiling and was longer than the first, the far end was dimly looped in darkness.

By now one or two were beginning to hold hands, making their candles wobble, sending out weird revolving shadows on the rough walls. Still we pressed on, shuffling a little now, our arms becoming stiff and tired. Hot flecks of wax stung our hands as the candles began to drip. Soon we could see another tiny hole and it was obvious that only the smallest of us could wriggle through. A noticeable lifting of the spirits bubbled up in those who couldn't possibly be asked to go on, their sense of adventure melting away with the candle wax.

So finally there were just the three of us, dogged pink June, myself and John.

By now we had lost interest in what we might actually find in these empty dark chambers, it was rather a matter of finishing something we had started. Once we were through the hole, the ceiling was so low that we were completely bent double. Three candles only gave much less light than ten—and crouching so low, as we were, it was almost impossible to see where we were going. Our backs brushed the roof and dust sprayed over us. We could feel it in our hair and trickling down our collars. Our noses, hair, and eyes became filled with it in the dark unending tunnel.

I became overwhelmed with terror. We were going to be buried alive. For the first time I was aware of other scratching noises as we disturbed spiders and beetles in the crannies of bricks. They had probably been blissfully unaware that such things as humans existed. They fell on us and ran over us, as we jolted them abruptly from their peaceful silence. I was rigid with fear, but while the others inched their way along, I couldn't stop moving, like a link in an unstoppable conveyor belt. Suddenly I was jerked to a halt. John who was in front had stopped. I tried to ask why, but couldn't form the words, my whole body felt useless.

"That's the end".

A very slight hum of distant traffic reached our straining ears from a tiny grating. No light came through, it was set so close to the ground. John was poking his fingers through the ornamental metal grid but there was nothing more to be found. We had passed from one side of the house to the other and now the three of us were wedged like toothpaste in the end of the tube. We stayed like that for a while, ruminating silently and getting our breath back. At least we more or less knew where we were and this was, in its way, quite some comfort. There were no demons nor decomposing corpses to be dealt with.

We had just to get back to the others. I was no longer afraid of the unknown, it was the known now that squeezed my ribs, my shoulders, my screwed up legs, with horror at our situation. I didn't want to breathe. It made my body larger and pressed it even more tightly against the encasing coffin of the roof. The candles had fallen and gone out some time since and of course we were facing the wrong way. Without any word or even conscious reasoning, sure instinct drove my legs out from under me. I pushed them hard behind, the earth fell away in lumps. I pulled at June and tugged at her ankles, in this fashion the three of us wriggled wildly backwards on our tummies. Then I could hear the others, nervous and squeaking. I felt my feet being dragged through the gap in the wall. My dress came right up over my shoulders and the folds of the material wound themselves around my neck and mouth. Frantically I scrabbled the rest of my body out of the hole. Gulping for air, gasping with frenzy more than effort, I tore myself free from certain death. Knowing what I felt like made me frantic to get the other two out.

June lay on the ground for a while and John swayed and stumbled about blindly, looking sickly green in the dying candlelight. We three were not inclined to say anything much.

"Let's go back".

With one accord we followed, meek and docile. By the time we reached the first cellar we had recovered our energy and our spirits. We were fairly safe, we could properly savour the last few minutes of the occasion.

Sitting cross-legged in a circle, we passed around three apples, the hairy bread and a couple of biscuits. Each took a bite and passed it on to the next person. This ritual communion revived us considerably. Several even leapt to their feet and chased their own shadows on the rough cast wall. Dancing round and around, wheeling and aeroplaning until they were dizzy and the bursts of light and dark came spinning and arching above and below transforming the cellar into a glittering funfair. A little magic spell was cast upon the dank gloomy cellar. Just a few stubs of candles remained and the leapers bobbed their blobs of flames still wider. Wildly kicking up the earth, they churned about in a final game of 'he', until exhaustion spilled them hot and breathless to the floor. All the candles had blown out and the bits were lost in the blackness, only the still silent John held the last flicker. Scrambling and falling over each other we dragged ourselves out into the summer moonlight and the sighing swishing grass.

A painful hush spread among us as we crouched on the bottom step and watched the boys crawl up the stairs on all fours and disappear through the French windows of the dining room. By the time we reached our dormitories we were leaning tiredly on each other, holding hands and whining gently about our grazes and filthy condition.

The following day we all appeared uniformly dirty, but our appearance was not commented upon and the entire episode was soon forgotten.

Learning Lessons

In between times in these busy days there was the small matter of the actual lessons.

I was at school in the heyday of the eleven plus but I don't remember ever feeling unduly concerned about my future prospects. The world outside The Elms was so vague and mysterious that I had no real idea of the difference between one school and another. I plodded along from day to day, doing as I was bid without the slightest inkling of my academic standard or progress.

Playing was more important than work and lessons filled up the spaces between playtimes. In the squashed somnolence of the schoolroom there was nothing else to do except think your private thoughts or get on with your work. Nothing was any great trial to me, except arithmetic. In common with legions of small children, I toiled over rods, poles, perches, fathoms, acres, etc., all to no avail. My poor little brain turned to stone when confronted by multiplying £19.17s & 10¾d by £3.19s.5¼d. Numbers jiggled up and down in front of me while I did multitudinous calculations without having a clue as to what I was doing.

The second Miss Meadmore, the queen of the classroom, left me in no doubt that I was as dull as a plank and I had to agree with her, I was. Most children exist in a non-mathematical world and however hard teachers may try to make Maths relevant, it just isn't. A child's mind is not rooted in the same kind of reality as an adult. Most children couldn't care two hoots how long anything is or how heavy etc. A meticulous analysis of order, pattern or relativity held no fascination for me until I was quite grown up, when suddenly I realised how absorbing such puzzles could be, just for their own sake. But I had to have experienced far more of life and living and developed that particular kind of analytical perception before the mathematical world opened up to me. Then a marvellous kind of wonder dawned upon me at the vast body of mathematical language and invention that is the framework and construction of mankind's civilised existence. No one could have provoked that realisation artificially, it needed time to grow as I grew. Bits and pieces just lobbed at you here and there didn't belong to a recognisable whole and there appeared no rhyme or reason for me to remember them.

Certain activities stick in my mind that must have occupied a deal of my attention and also continued for a lengthy period of time. Nature loomed large in our school lives. At nine years old my knowledge of birds and names of wild flowers was quite extensive. I can't remember any of it now unfortunately, which irks me. It's like a familiar tune that you just can't quite name.

We used to make large calendars on white drawing paper with a big square for each day. Around the squares the border was decorated with flowers, trees, insects, birds, appropriate to the coming month. In the squares we would write about anything we saw on our daily perambulations around the park. If we couldn't go out then we wrote about what we could see from the window or in the garden. These little 'nature notes' could be anything from details about the weather, to the first snowdrop, or the new moon or even the doings of the hedgehogs.

At one time the Meadmores fed two hedgehogs they christened Bryant and May. We knew which was which because May had, at some time, had an encounter with some green paint and had a fancy green flash down one side. Saucers of bread soaked in milk were put out for Bryant and May and we lay in wait by the playroom window for their arrival. They were quite celebrities at The Elms for a while and we patiently hung around for ages just to catch a quick glimpse of them in the furthest reaches of the light from the playroom, mooching around their saucer. It was probably those calendars that encouraged us to be so aware of the teeming natural world around us. We did not come from a generation where you shrugged your shoulders and blithely declared 'I don't know what to write'. When instructed to write something in each square, you jolly well did write something. Even if it meant poking the ground to see if there were any worms about.

'The earth smelt nice after the rain', or 'The grass has grown and needs cutting'. No detail was too minuscule to be recorded. Even the wretched cats were mentioned in dispatches. We hunted for the first buds, the first cuckoo, the first leaf to fall, the first snowflake. We measured how much the roses had grown in a month and the exact colours of each variety were agonisingly and precisely recorded.

This went on every day for a whole year.

Even in the holidays you had to keep your notes and fill in the empty squares when you came back to school. Nobody did keep notes of course, we just made it up. 'Went to the zoo and saw lions and tigers'. 'Had a thunder storm and the house next door was struck by lightning'. 'Our dog died today'. These and other terse little comments enlivened the proceedings. We swapped notes and found it hugely entertaining to see who could invent the most improbable story and actually get away with it. It couldn't be too fantastic, it needed to be more or less believable so that if pounced on to explain the incident you could dredge up a plausible explanation. In spite of the drawbacks I enjoyed those calendars particularly and they made a great impression on me. Which wasn't surprising, because at the end of a year, I had twelve of them all neatly bound together. They contained a wealth of curious information and they looked quite impressive with their colourfully decorated borders. Of course as part of this mammoth exercise, we were carefully trained to draw wild flowers which was a satisfying accomplishment.

I wasn't often satisfied with my achievements but I liked drawing and painting and sweated blood over my tulips, rabbits or blackberries until I was pleased with the results.

In my era, needlework was given some prominence on the curriculum for boys and girls, and they were so pernickety you felt you were being trained to be a court dressmaker. Little fingers get hot and sticky so although I quite liked sewing and embroidery it was never as neat as I wished it to be and often ended up a suspicious soggy grey colour. There was only one object of which I was inordinately proud and that was a fairly large needlecase made of different coloured pieces of felt in the shape of Red Riding Hood except it was blue. It was in several layers. You lifted up the cloak and there was an apron and under the apron was a dress and so on. Each layer contained different sized needles and a thimble fitted into the basket on the outside. The figure was completed by a bonnet edged with flowers, a velvet collar and pink felt legs and blue boots. I gave it to Nanny as a Christmas present when it was finished. I nearly burst with pride when she unwrapped it and for years it hung on a hook on the dresser and the little legs used to dangle and swing in the constant drought from the scullery.

There were the inevitable copperplate handwriting sessions. I religiously enscribed 'Opium comes from poppies' about nine hundred times in the course of my six years at The Elms without having the faintest idea what opium was. There would be a public outcry and headlines in the press if juniors were asked to write this today. Handwriting was a pleasantly mindless task with which to finish a school day and no one objected. Both the Meadmores had quite unbelievably perfect handwriting themselves. It looked almost as though it had been printed on a machine. They would weep if they saw mine now, especially after the amount of paper and ink that was expended on it.

Another popular task was learning poetry, good old chestnuts like 'Daffodils' and 'Cargoes' and 'John Gilpin'. We would stand in a line and intone these. Or joy of joys, we might be asked to say them alone. Inevitably I have remembered them all of my life. Often I would learn others from *A Child's Garden of Verse* at home, just because I wanted to know poems I liked by heart, so I could say them to myself sometimes. These were the days before television or sophisticated toys, and poetry was a form of entertainment to me. Nanny often used to recite poems she had learned as a child. 'Maud Muller' was one, but my favourite was 'The Children's Hour'.

Between the dark and the daylight,
when the night is beginning to lower,
comes a pause in the day's occupations,
which is known as the children's hour.

It always sounded so safe and warm and loving. 'Grave Alice, laughing Allegra and Edith with golden hair', curled up on a rug in front of a blazing fire listening to their grandfather's stories. There weren't many books at school, so you learnt things by heart, because you read the same ones over and over again. Another absolute favourite book was *The Wind in the Willows*, which sustained me for years. It's not surprising that it took me so long to establish any contact with my 20th century contemporaries, when most of my imaginative life was so deeply rooted in the last century.

A certain amount of rudimentary geography was presented to us in the form of 'children from other lands'. Vague memories of painting friezes of happy villagers in coolie hats paddling about in paddy fields float before me. Or perhaps we did that at Sunday School in London I can't be sure. But at some point I was happily occupied painting long narrow friezes. Indians on the banks of the Bhramaputra in gaily coloured sari's have stuck fast to my memory.

I have no recollection of any religious education, but we were conscientiously dispatched, in a 'crocodile' to the local church every Sunday. It was a lovely old church with a lovely old vicar to match. He had rather wayward grey hair and a kindly ruddy face that was thin and lined. He always spoke to us after the service and occasionally bobbed up at school for no particular reason that we could see. The pews in the church were the big old oak variety and we had a special one that we were always directed to. It was so big that we could duck down inside it and get lost for most of the service.

I wonder now if the Meadmores were not religiously inclined, because neither of them ever came to church with us. It was always Miss Polsue or Miss Metcalfe. Also, when we were being castigated for our constant wrong doing, there was never any mention of sin or damnation. (It was Nanny who forever reminded me of how wicked and sinful I was.) The Christmas and Easter festivals passed without any reference to them in our lessons. So I conclude that my junior education must have been fairly secular.

There was no assembly, no hymns, no nativity scenes or any picture or book around the school with any religious significance. Only in the lounge on the mantelpiece was a small painting of the head of the Madonna. It showed a very young sweet-faced girl in the traditional light blue veil with her eyes downcast. The story was that it was painted by David Kossoff. Which was odd, because he's a Jew, and I don't think he was on more friendly terms with the Meadmore's than any other parent. So I wonder why he gave it to her? Anyway Miss Meadmore (one) was very proud of this painting and, when parents arrived, the picture would be introduced into the conversation at the earliest appropriate moment.

Towards the end of my years at The Elms a French teacher appeared. Mademoiselle Lapin. She was slim and dark-haired and years younger than the other teachers. Our attention was rivetted on her, not because she was French, or even because she was young, but because she had the most astonishingly pointed breasts. They looked like little spears poking through the thin blouses that she always wore. Contemporary ladies underwear was quite unknown territory to all us little girls and we were agog with curiosity. Was she really that shape? Was there something fresh to be discovered about the female anatomy beyond our own stubby little bodies and the wildly bolstered Meadmores? We acquired a few French phrases about opening doors and closing windows, but it was those spiky hatpin breasts that made the most lasting impression on me.

And so it was with the rest of my official education, a conglomeration of impressions and the odd fact tossed into the rushing stream of childhood. I don't think it would have been much different in another school. Elementary skills like reading, writing and computation improve with regular practice, but knowledge builds up slowly and unconsciously and is totally dependant on mood and attitude and a host of other immeasurable factors beyond any educator's control.

The ruminative silence of the classroom encouraged concentration, but even then more often than not, my thoughts drifted off into a thousand different directions. The vivid private life of a child will ever confound those sorry souls whose job it is to command their reluctant attention.

Each term each season brought fresh fields of interest and new preoccupations. A bicycle appeared one day and everyone took turns learning to ride, with varying degrees of of success. When it was my turn I went almost purple with the effort, but I never managed more than a few turns of the wheels before I was face down in the dirt. My struggles ended in a spectacular conclusion when someone gave me a mighty shove. I wobbled uncontrollably for a few feet and as I felt myself falling yet again, I grabbed frantically for the nearest object to hang on to. Unfortunately it was a very large water butt filled with rain water. I missed the edge and literally dived in head first. Miraculously my feet became wedged in the pedals so I only went in up to my waist. The others tugged at my clothes and fished me out spluttering and yelping, plucking at moving water, frantic for something solid to grip on to and so lever myself out of the butt. I was sent to bed at 4.00 p.m. and had a long time to reflect that riding bicycles caused drowning. Although I did try again on other occasions, to my shame I have never learned to ride a bike or control anything on wheels. But I did become quite good at doing things on two feet or even two hands.

The high spot of every week for me was Saturday morning. From the age of five when I first came to The Elms I had taken ballet lessons as an 'extra'. These lessons were my total and absolute joy. I adored everything about them. The music, the exercises, the acrobatics. This was my world where I felt I was mistress of the situation. In so many other things, it was like the bicycle running away from under me, throwing me where it chose—usually the ground.

Miss Smithers, my teacher, was lovely and gave me years of the wonderful wonderful feeling of being good at something. I never aspired to actually becoming a dancer—my mother would have found it too difficult to organise her life around me and my interests. In the end Miss Smithers trained me for the Wells 'entrance', but I never actually went to the audition at Sadler's Wells. It was quite beyond my wildest imaginings that I would really ever get there. I knew even then that I didn't come from that kind of family. But I was thrilled that Miss Smithers had even considered me worth the effort of training as she did, and that she thought I was good enough to go for an audition.

Eventually it became a lifetime's hobby and passionate interest. I realised later that Miss Smithers was an excellent teacher, who had instilled a pure classical Russian style. Those Saturday morning lessons were austere almost to the point of masochism. When I left The Elms and searched for another ballet teacher, I was quite mystified to discover it was all ringlets, bitching, satin ribbons and coveys of mums. Navy knickers, a vest and ballet shoes were all we had, we were merely supplicants to the dance.

The lessons were held in a largeish wooden hall that stood on bricks by the side of the rose garden. Our feet shushed and bounced on the greyish dirty wooden floorboards to the unvarying routine of the five positions' warm-up exercises. Miss Smithers walked around carefully placing our heads, arms, feet, shoulders, to the exact position she required. We went over and over these exercises until we could do them in our sleep. As we grew tired, so she drove us harder— to hold ourselves up ever higher, ever more lightly and show no strain or fatigue. Our breathing had to be carefully practised so we never panted or became breathless. From the standing positions we progressed to the bar. Our backs were held straight as boards, as we kick-ed our legs forward, back, sideways, changing our direc-tions fluently and without a break. Plié, developpé, frappé, fouetté, chânge-mânge— these words became absorbed into my daily vocabulary. Glissard, glissard, pas de bas, pas de bas, we followed Miss Smither's recitations faithfully, we were her acolytes.

Little dances and routines were slowly built up over the years. At the end of each lesson was a glorious session of acrobatics and Miss Smithers sent us all off dirty but ex-hilarated. In spite of all our effort, in those two hours of non-stop physical exercise (you were never permitted to rest, relax, or slump in any way on pain of being turned into a sack of potatoes), we were not particularly tired. But we did have a raging thirst, having breathed so much of the dust from the ancient wooden hall. Jostling and pushing each other we thrust our heads under taps and poured water down our throats. When we had changed we tore across to the dining room. Like eager puppies impatient for the din-ner gong to sound, we sniffed the glorious smells from the kitchen. Bobbing up and down we formed a disorderly queue outside the door, each one determined to be first in the dinner line.

One year Miss Smithers prepared her little band for a 'dancing display'. This was to be held in a nearby hall and parents and teachers were invited to watch. For weeks beforehand we spent hours stitching hooks and eyes on our tutus. Sad Miss Polsue supervised the sewing and was impossible to satisfy. I sewed hooks on and Miss Polsue ripped them off. I'm sure this happened a hundred times—I just couldn't get my blasted stitches neat enough. The cotton became grey and greasy as I laboriously sweated over my task, getting evermore hot and flustered each time she ripped off the hook. Somehow the sewing was finished without a great deal of thanks to me.

The Elms was, in its modest way, quite a little furnace of romance and my affections centred upon a small pale little boy called Robin Robinson. Whom I called 'Wobin Wobinson'. At this time I was quite unable to sound the letter 'R'. My mother found tales of 'Wobin' highly amusing and I was pleased by her merriment. However this impediment I found distinctly less enchanting as I grew older. 'Wobin' was my dancing partner and for the display we were to perform a little dance together. My robust little body was encased in my tutu and, due to the hundred and one wretched hooks and eyes, once I was in it, it was impossible to get me out. Unfortunately 'Wobin' was not so lucky. Someone's burst of imagination had devised for him a velvet suit of a particularly bilious green. The trousers ended just past the knees and were tapered to fit tightly above his non-existent calf muscles. The jacket didn't quite reach as far as the top of the trousers, so a crimson sash was found to plug the gap between jacket and trousers.

This ensemble was completed by a frilly shirt with lace ruffles down the front and at the cuff. The shirt was miles too big and the jacket very small. The only things that actually fitted were his long white socks and dancing pumps, because these were his own. The waist of the trousers did not have a proper band and the material was a bit flimsy. Well, his many dressers, including me, pushed and pulled and poked and tucked until he looked a bit roly poly but fairly presentable. He must have been an astoundingly placid child, because he made no protest at being trussed into these curious garments.

While he stood quite still waiting for his big moment, with me furiously scraping his hair behind his ears, all seemed well. Our few bars of introductory music were played, the pianist beamed at us and on we ran to greet our audience. Of course it took just a few energetic steps for poor 'Wobin' to completely disintegrate. He gently unravelled in all directions. It hardly took a minute for his trousers to slide down and dangle over his knees and my fingers to become enmeshed in his lacy cuffs. I tugged furiously and what looked like half a mile of shirt emerged from inside his jacket sleeve. Like a great ape his arms dragged on the floor. The vast shirt began to avalanche back and front and nearly bury him. I was so cross; I dragged that poor uncomplaining little boy back to the wings. The audience tittered sympathetically as they watched me cobble him back together again with huge safety pins supplied by the still beaming pianist.

When I was satisfied that his trousers wouldn't actually fall down, I heaved the great winding sheet of a shirt right off his back and bundled him back onto the floor. We completed our little number with 'Wobin' in his vest and I was satisfied. We must have looked like an infant adagio act— all I needed was a striped jersey and a beret. My hooks and eyes held like rocks throughout all of this furious activity. I should have been grateful to poor Miss Polsue, but of course I wasn't. 'Wobin' appeared bemused but none the worse for his experience and he never held it against me afterwards.

The first Miss Meadmore sat slap bang in the middle of the front row. She was wearing a brown outdoor coat and looked like a huge armchair. I had never seen her in outdoor clothes before. I never saw either of the Meadmores go out at all, to me they were part of the structure of the house. They held the place up like buttresses. She was, on this occasion, wearing her strangely maniac smile that remained fixed as though carved on her face throughout the whole proceedings. The rest of the evening passed in a pleasant flurry of petticoats and the warm hum of chatter in the drawing-room.

There were other missed entrances, steps forgotten, and shoes and hats that flew unerringly into the laps of the audience. However, no one was at all perturbed by these spontaneous occurrences, evidently it all added to audience's enjoyment. At the end everyone congratulated everyone else. Tea, biscuits and orange juice were served and a wonderful time was had by all.

We never had another dancing 'display'.

Home

Home was a place to go to, to escape the unpleasantness of school. On the other hand school was a place to escape the unpleasantness of home.

I eventually grew up without a strong sense of 'home'. Wherever I was, if I felt O.K., that was home. Home was a place inside myself. I never missed anybody and I never missed any place.

I always felt twice the size, once I was inside our front door. After school our house was like a cupboard. There was the same dark brown paint everywhere and brown cracked linoleum on the floor. It was just as draughty, but once we were inside the kitchen with a fire burning in the range and our chairs drawn up around it, with the blind and curtains closed, it could be quite cozy. The table took up most of the space and a small sideboard and four chairs took up the rest. There was just about enough room to walk in and out. During the day the door between the kitchen and scullery was left open and we moved between the two for our various occupations. At night the door was closed and we were sealed in for the evening.

Nanny was a reluctant housekeeper and most domestic duties were performed to the letter rather than the spirit. I suppose there was precious little to encourage her, but homemaking was definitely a chore and not a pleasure.

Floors were swept and clothes were washed and ironed as necessary, but she was never inspired to change or renew anything to make the house more comfortable. High-backed wooden chairs and dreary coloured everything from walls to floor was the established order. And so it remained until I left her when I was about sixteen.

Nanny was the child of immigrant parents, born, I believe somewhere near Leipzig. I wish I had questioned her more closely about their exact origin, but it never occurred to me when I was small. By the time I became interested in these historic details it was too late. Her collection of odd little words and phrases and strange pronunciations I took as part and parcel of the curious package that was Nanny. I knew that she was rather peculiar and that I was, by this association, 'different' from my friends.

This difference embarrassed me and so I kept it as quiet as possible— especially, I kept quiet about it to myself. When I was at boarding school we were all in the same boat. Hardly any of us had two real parents and for those who did they were either abroad or lived so far away they didn't count anyway. Once I went to day school, however, this 'difference' became more apparent and I loathed it and yearned to be the 'same'. It was not just Nanny's foreignness that caused my difference, she lived, breathed, and dreamed a bygone age. An age into which she tried to push and shove me, but I just didn't fit.

She was, I eventually decided, considered a beauty in her youth, with very sloping shoulders, full bosom, strong features and thick wavy dark brown hair. While my mother and I had curves about as voluptuous as string beans. Nevertheless when the time came, we still had to be poured into corsets once we out grew our liberty bodices. These garments of female torture we most certainly did not need. We were Nanny's despair, and our offending thinness had to be shrouded by garments from neck to ankle and thus concealed.

My natural inclination towards athleticism was even

more appalling. However much she poked and prodded me and threw up her hands, I was not to be the graceful swan of the officer's drill hall that she had been. In the event I turned out to be a fairly good fit for the rock and roll generation I was rightfully born into.

Nanny lived inside a Strauss waltz and tempestuous outbursts and prima donna gestures were all part of the performance. She loved resigning from things. I think she only joined her various societies in order to resign dramatically at a later date. I learned a lot about Lily Langtry, Sarah Bernhardt, all the Royal Family, most especially Princess Alexandra. All these ladies rolled into one were Nanny, floating round and round an everlasting ballroom inside the waltz. I'm sure her dream was to be offered the throne on the stage of Drury Lane. After graciously accepting it, she would promptly resign and hurl the crown at the feet of an adoring populace, who would plead with her to return and be their Queen.

To relive all this after a distance of years is hugely entertaining. But to be a child right up close to these obsessions and complexities was very disturbing.

Nanny's storms filled the house, her whole body could be ravaged by tears. Life with her was an emotional minefield. The smallest disturbance could trigger these tremendous explosions. Her tragic cry of 'four walls, four walls' echoes down the years. It was her pleading and craving for some kind of stardom or recognition... She wished to be conveyed in carriages drawn by horses with plumes to glittering balls and receptions where she would be fêted for her wondrous talents and great person. Nanny was a frustrated 'great lady', imprisoned in her tiny cell of a house, fettered by unwelcome domesticity. All these passions and yearnings eddied around me. I caught the last violent convulsions of years dedicated to high drama. I missed her 'hey day' of being a church warden's wife at St. Michael's where she ruled over her kingdom with capricious tyranny and did battle with her rivals in the Mother's Union. There, she and she alone, if she could help it, would organize any passing young curates and be the handmaiden most worshipped and relied upon of the incumbent vicar of the moment. And woe betide anyone who dared to come between Nanny and her self-importance. These tales of St. Michael's were related to me, usually with photographs of outings, rambles and fêtes— it sounded more like the Court of England than the Church of England or even Camelot. But by the time I was on the scene she had long since resigned from all these exalted positions.

Having no doubt created havoc in all her spheres of interest and having left a trail of debris of bad feeling behind her, I was now the focus of a lifetime of discontent and bitter resentment. I was the only subject left in her kingdom for her to rule.

When you are a very young child it doesn't occur to you to question the way things are. What is, is— it is the only world you know. I was very frightened when Nanny twisted her face into a grotesque grimace and shrieked "I hate you, I hate you", pushing her face right into mine. As she cried and raved, I cried too, "I'm sorry, I'm sorry", believing completely that whatever was wrong was all my fault. Once she had provoked a sufficiently strong emotional response from me, then she was satisfied and her rage would subside.

My grandfather had been a kindly, gentle very good man and my mother had inherited his temperament. Both of them had coaxed, cajoled and coped with Nanny's wayward nature for years. They managed to continue with their daily lives by working their way around her, just for a quiet life.

Only occasionally would they seriously flout her wishes. However, I was not kindly, gentle and good. I was strong willed and as determined as she was.

The more she tried to repress me, the more it fed my determination not to be repressed. To the utter despair of my poor mother, the older I grew, the more frequently I would stand my ground and fight Nanny to the death almost. Usually over something quite staggeringly trivial, like knickers or hair ribbons.

I was quite impossible when it came to my clothes. I liked things to match and look nice. Humpy, bumpy, ugly ill fitting garments drove me to a distraction equal to her own. She sometimes made me dresses that looked as charming as a warehouseman's overalls. Of course, the plain truth was that Nanny and I were very much like. My vanity and self seeking matched her own. Nanny's emotionalism gave me free rein to be exactly the same.

The dramas and scenes I grew accustomed to and were not seriously debilitating. They became almost a ritual and in time Nanny had to learn to placate me. My own well of tears was as deep as her own. She possessed that rich sentimentality and angst of the Central European that Anglo Saxons find so alarming, but I was possessed of it too.

So in some strange uncomprehending way I understood her when others did not. Consequently there were many pleasures that we could share. She was enormously musical and often played the piano. Viennese music was her joy and light operetta. 'The Maid of the Mountains' and Ivor Novello I remember especially. In her youth she had sung on a concert platform and she loved to sing. One of my favourites was a little song called 'Gross mutter', which I think reminded her of her mother, who had been 'a sweet apple cheeked lady'.

When the radio played her favourite music she and I would dance in the minute space in the kitchen, quite carried away by the lilting melodies that held so many precious dreams for her. I shared those moments, almost as if I too had worn tarlatan dresses and danced with the officers at the drill hall. A sparkling gaiety would fill her entire being and she would laugh coquettishly, her hands raised, her fingers drifting gracefully through the air. Her head tilted away, smiling coquettishly at some imaginary admirer. She would be lost in her delicious reverie.

At those times I egged her on to tell me about her girlish adventures with her sister 'Sissy'. Of how they made their dresses and prepared for weeks for those special occasions. When they would creep out of the house secretly so their brutal drunken father would not know and their dear mother would let them in very quietly when they returned. But the best story was the one about the "Squire of Groombridge', who had gazed directly into her eyes when she played the piano while he sang a plaintive Victorian ditty. This had been at some Christmas soirée she and Grandad had attended. Every detail of that evening she described to me right down to the scarlet velvet of the rose given her by the squire, and she delighted in my wrapt attention. Often in those long evenings we spent together I would chirp "Tell me again, Nanny, tell me about the Squire of Groombridge".

We would listen to the radio, to 'Sunday Night at Eight', 'Henry Hall' or 'In Town Tonight', while we played Crib or 'Gin Rummy'.

She taught me to sew, knit and embroider, both of us sitting on straight high-backed chairs opposite each other at the kitchen table, enjoying Ted Ray or Arthur Askey. Nanny's crochet work was legendary, but I was never to rise to such lofty heights of creation with those delicate balls of white silk. Sometimes she would teach me one of her Old Tyme Dances in the square inch of floor by the door.

Dancing was one of her passions and all three of us went regularly to Old Tyme dances. Dressing up for these occasions was lovely and Nanny would dance with my mother and me in turn. There were various cronies we would meet at the dances and they were usually jolly good natured affairs. Nanny was a good dancer and saw herself as queen of the dance floor. She would push my poor mother around, who was rather awkward with little natural rhythm, and get terribly jealous if any of the men danced with her, or in any way paid her small attentions. At these moments Nanny would dance with me and I was grateful for the chance to get on the dance floor. Of course she always had to lead, but I didn't mind because I could do them all as easily as she could. In fact I knew quite well that I was better than her, because I actually enjoyed the dancing. If I made a mistake I would concentrate very hard until I got it right. Nanny spent too much time showing off and frequently got in a muddle if a new dance was being taught. Often I would show her how to do it when we were at home.

The dances were not wholly as pleasant as they might have been because someone in the company would usually err at some point and fall from grace and Nanny would become techy. She was always forthright in stating her views and opinions but she was deeply offended, not to say totally outraged, if anyone else had the temerity to do the same thing. She didn't really have friends, she preferred absolute subservience.

Another of her great loves were 'outings', coach trips particularly. We visited all kinds of places, in spite of my suffering quite badly from travel sickness. I was topped up with greaseproof paper bags and a Kwell and we would sally forth. I have been sick in all kinds of interesting places. I couldn't have minded that much, because I can't remember not wanting to go on these outings. The only time I really dreaded it was when we had a ten or twelve hour journey to the North of England to visit Uncle Eddie and Aunty Alice, which we did quite frequently. Eddie was Nanny's son who had wisely moved to Darlington after the war.

Positively the worst journey I can recall was a trip by coach to Cornwall which took fifteen hours, I really thought my end had come. We had arrived at Victoria Coach station at some ungodly hour like seven and we were still sitting on that damned coach at about eleven o'clock that night. It took so long I thought we had travelled thousands of miles. These were pre-motorway days and when you arrived at your destination it felt as if you were in another country. Everything was so strange and different. After a long journey you had a much stronger sensation of having travelled a great distance to somewhere excitingly novel.

Nanny liked travelling and was surprisingly resilient to any long waits or other discomforts the journey might entail. An expedition crammed with incident was retold with as much relish as an uneventful one. She would sink like a dying swan, clutch her bosom make gasping noises, and fan herself as if she had driven a team of horses single handed from the banks of the Vistula river.

Her pleasures were felt as intensely as her sorrows and frustrations. In spite of her outbrusts against the inhumanity of her existence, really she led a very full life. Church fêtes, bazaars, bring and buy sales, dances, parish parties and suchlike activities littered my childhood. Wherever she went I trotted along with her. Most of the events took place in dusty friendly church halls with dusty friendly people.

Interspersed among this crowded calender, Nanny regularly indulged in her other great delight, which was the cinema— another passion we had in common. Cinema-going during the war and postwar years was a national pastime. After a jolly good row that had run its natural course we would put on our hats and coats, make our sandwiches and quite matily repair to the Dominion. Sadly, gone are those vast audiences that filled every corner of those 'gorgeous palaces of pleasure'. They made up that very special atmosphere that was an essential part of the joy of going to the 'pictures'. Warmth, music and life combined to swell hearts in one great joyous surge of conviviality. After walking through damp silent, grey streets the bright shining lights of the foyer welcomed you in to an exciting adventurous place. Painted walls gleamed and carpet softened your tread. When I was very young I was devoted to Roy Rogers (or Woy Wogers, as I called him), but I progressed to Robert Taylor and Dana Andrews or whoever was Nanny's current favourite. I wasn't fussy who it was, I'd have sat through a history of aerodynamics and happily munched my paste sandwiches if required. Happily, Nanny's taste was for romances, historical dramas and musicals which suited me very well. Especially, I loved musicals with Gene Kelly and Frank Sinatra.

To sail away into a technicolour dreamland, sitting in the one and threes so close to the screen, as if you were right inside the film with the stars, was the next best thing to heaven. Pretty people charmingly warbling away about small dilemmas that were always happily resolved at the end of the picture. It was the most soothing balm in an uncomfortable world. Goodies were good and baddies were bad, the stories made sense and nice people were nice to each other. Villains got their just desserts. Surely there must have been crowds of us whose entire ideal of human behaviour was shaped by such films and books, striving desperately to make our own lives fit this simple pattern.

Of course I knew in my heart none of those things were true, but at the same time it was comforting to feel that someone came home to a lovely house with ever-blazing fires, soft carpet and deep welcoming settees . For those few hours in a darkened cinema you shared that cozy existence and vicariously lived the lives of those ever-beautiful people. I never craved to be a film star, because I didn't really appreciate that they were ordinary people just pretending. My absolute dream was to live in the story. Inevitably I loved stories about families, especially turn of the century American families.

However humble they were supposed to be they always lived in wondrously large rambling houses with swings, rocking chairs and hammocks in extensive gardens. If it was winter they built snowmen and played snowballs in fur bonnets and were welcomed home with steaming glasses of hot punch prepared by some devoted old retainer. Loving relationships abounded and provided strength and comfort during their various trials and sorrows. 'Little Women' and 'Meet me in St. Louis' became my romantic blueprint for living.

During these times Nanny and I rubbed along quite amicably and I probably saw her at her best. So many of our interests and talents were similar that we could have been happy together. I was usually amenable to anything she wanted to do and I learned a great deal from her. Nearly every evening we were together because my mother had her own life and friends whom she went out with.

Apart from church or Sunday school, an outing with my mother was a rare treat and I was always absolutely on my best behaviour. I daren't be anything other than angelic in case she never took me out again. I rather held her on a pedestal. Because Nanny had almost sole charge of me she was in my eyes a mundane figure who did boring things like washing and shopping. My mother was the good fairy who appeared occasionally and whisked me away to pantomimes and the ballet and other exciting places, followed by lovely rolls and butter with cups of tea in Lyons Corner House. This was really living. In spite of this Nanny and I were more fundamentally alike.

My mother always appeared to inhabit a slightly rarefied atmosphere. She was deeply religious and very preoccupied with being good. Nanny and I were livelier and threw ourselves into everything with certain gusto, but we were certainly not good. She taught me a tremendous amount that I really enjoyed. Sadly this was not enough for her. Her enormously possessive and dominating nature destroyed what was a promising foundation. Instead of drawing us together, our similarity wrenched us apart. For in Nanny's schemes no one was permitted a single individual idea or solitary personal gesture. You had to sit, sleep eat, even breathe according to her wishes. There were good times and pleasant moments, but they were strictly on her terms, always. I was a splendid audience for all her tales and willing accomplice in any venture. My role was solely of a Victorian lady's companion, to be chivvied, nagged, bullied, according to her whim. Gaiety, good nature or frivolity were occasionally bestowed upon me if she happened to be feeling benevolent.

As a little child I merely wriggled in my straitjacket, but as I grew bigger that wriggling became a desperate struggle to break free of her. More and more I deliberately set out to be annoying. The harder I resisted the more strongly she tried to hold me down. So when the scenes and rages no longer worked the emotional blackmail began.

'How could I be so wicked after all she'd done for me?' 'How could I be so ungrateful?' 'Hadn't she taken me in when there was no where else to go?'

This litany was repeated ad nauseam and for a while it worked, like all her little ploys. For I knew she had done a great deal for me and I relied on her utterly.

She was the strength of the home, always the one who took charge of things in any crisis. For a while I would acquiesce, also to please my mother who hated there to be any trouble when she came home from work. The nagging went on. I was flayed alive by Nanny's constant stream of criticism, as though my flesh was being stripped to the bone. Nothing I could say or do would please her. Finally all the tales had been told, all the songs sung. Nanny, as a source of entertainment and companionship, had exhausted herself. Even these small shared pleasures had been chewed up and spat out.

By the time I was about twelve and attending the local grammar school, I sought my interests and companions elsewhere.

More and more Nanny would have 'attacks' and 'funny turns'. She had been dying since she was thirty five and if she didn't get her own way, would regularly sway dramatically and clutch her heart. She would 'faint' and fall comfortably onto the floor, her body suitably arranged to achieve the best effect. When she considered she had our full attention she would breathe heavily and lisp 'brandy, brandy'. Her eyes would roll as she apparently struggled to regain consciousness. For years she had been perfecting this little act and everyone knew it for what it was. But there was always that gnawing fear in the back of your mind that perhaps she really was ill, so we played along, moistening her lips with the requested brandy. Miraculously she would be restored to health by the healing process of me dancing attendance upon her. My heart hardened as I grew up and began to see her clearly as an autocratic tyrannical despot.

Once I had established other friendships her hold over me began to wane, her power was no longer total. My friend Maxine lived a few streets away and I would often go there, happy in her comfortable pleasant Warner's flat. No longer did I feel it was always me that was at fault, so I became more and more difficult for her to control. Threats of suicide became more frequent. She was always going to throw herself into the river Lea, or under a train or gas herself. These protestations fell on deaf ears. Cushions would be placed in the oven and towels draped under the door. So I would find her kneeling with her head inside the oven when I came home from school. Wearily I would pick her up and sort her out.

I learned to deal with her. The scenes and 'turns' became just a regular part of daily life like putting out the milk bottles. In her turn she came to realize that she had to deal with me. In this fashion we achieved a kind of equilibrium. But of course it was not to last.

Jill

Going back to school required a certain amount of preparation. My uniform had to be made ready, any new clothes I needed had to be bought. I was kitted out in dark navy blue from head to toe including the much hated thick navy blue socks. Sensible shoes were packed and liberty bodices, mammoth pairs of knickers and vests that reached my knees—not one frill, flounce or touch of colour could be seen inside that suitcase. Everything was large enough to allow for growing. My belted navy raincoat would have accommodated three little girls. During the last few days of the holiday, as I was being launched for another school term, it gave me time to consider the change from one life to another. So the transition from Lime Street to The Elms passed smoothly and I slid from my home self into my school self.

Scarcely pausing to say Goodbye I was packaged and bundled on to buses and underground trains and more buses. The only thing I knew with absolute certainty was that I was a long way away. Once I was deposited inside the door with my suitcase, it was as though that was all I had in the world, me and my suitcase.

I would hover uncertainly. I spent a lot of my childhood hovering uncertainly. Eventually I perfected the hovering technique while managing to conceal my anxiety. When you are more less in a constant state of having bewildering adult demands made on you, emotions become too confusing to register, so you register nothing. Impassivity becomes your norm. It gives you time to watch and take note. What do they want you to do? What do they want you to say? When a situation arises that seriously impinges upon, you a sudden response takes you totally by surprise and is regretted immediately.

Between my grandmother and the Meadmores I grew to be a rather watchful child, always weighing up the situation, ever wary of people's judgement of me, trying to bury myself as much as possible. On reflection this does not seem particularly unusual for children in my circumstance or my generation. For many of us at The Elms this kind of emotional isolation was quite normal and we became insulated by an inner creativity and resourcefulness. Pleasure and happiness could be distilled from a most unpromising or trifling experience. Each of us in our way coped with the hand dealt to us by circumstances. Although at the time our awareness of each other was vague and our common bond was one of need rather than true compatibility, occasionally the real sorrow of one of us came fleetingly to our attention.

Jill was a doctor's daughter, she came from Minehead or Hindhead we never discovered which. She was obviously used to something rather better than some of us. Lots of little things told us this. Printed name tags, a tailored uniform, soft towels, whiter underwear in a leather suitcase. All this spoke volumes even before we observed her manner and demeanour. Why she was there I have no idea. How long she was there I don't remember, but it couldn't have been long. She seemed part of a more settled and orderly existence. She didn't belong with us rag tag and bobtails. We were refugees from disorder, making the most of anything that came our way, adapting pliantly and bending with each changing wind.

Jill hated The Elms but never registered anything as

strong as hate. An awkward misery accompanied her each day. In the morning pink June and I rolled into our day clothes and perfunctorily straightened ourselves for the day ahead. Jill stood in her pyjamas, thick plaid woollen dressing gown and furry slippers, a sponge bag and towel in her hand. She trotted along the landing to the tiny sink in a recess by the toilet. The only bathroom was in the other house, where we were bathed once a week. To be bathed once a week was perfectly normal to me, for at home Friday night was bath night always in a tin bath in front of the kitchen range. To have a bathroom and toilet inside the house was unknown luxury.

But obviously Jill was used to better things. Everything about her seemed slower and more leisurely. We hurled our few possessions into drawers and cupboards, while she placed them carefully. Her shoes reposed side by side, not fifty yards apart, and her clothes remained in their appointed place on her body all day. She fell in with us and our various pursuits, but she was never quite one of us; she lived in the slip-stream of life at The Elms. Nothing about her behaviour caused anyone to take any particular notice of her. Whilst she bobbed along with the rest of us she displayed no especial liveliness or buoyancy. So when she announced one night in the bedroom that she was going to run away, we were all quite startled and amazed.

This interesting idea had never occurred to anyone before. Once the notion had taken shape and we had fully digested its implications, we were delighted. Of course it had to be done with all the proper ceremony and ritual laid down in all those 'boarding school' books with which we were all so familiar. Jill dressed herself in her outdoor clothes while we stripped the beds of all the sheets and solemnly struggled to knot them together. We more or less tied one end to the bedstead nearest the window and Jill dutifully clambered out on to the ledge without questioning the wisdom of such a foolhardy action. Once she was half in and half out of the window, with the sheets dangling over the side getting all caught up in the ivy, she realised that it was quite a long way down to the ground.

She swung her legs back inside the room and said she'd changed her mind. It was dark and rather windy and the kind of daring required for such an undertaking was not really in her nature. But Jill's courage went far beyond anything we could conceive.

"I think I'll just go downstairs and out of the back door."

Off she went and we didn't even say goodbye. For us the real enthusiasm was tying the sheets together, climbing down to the bottom and hurtling back up the stairs to safety. Breathlessly laughing and giggling at our own cleverness, we wouldn't have had the slightest idea what to do once we were actually out in the road alone. We played at climbing in and out of the window for a little while and then grew tired of the game and put all the sheets back on the beds.

By then we realised that Jill was not coming back. Our little adventures were just games. But Jill did not play games. She had a self possession and mature self confidence that was quite outside our understanding. We became nervous, real life had encroached upon our childhood territory and we didn't know what to do. At the same time we felt guilty for we were her accomplices. The enormity of our crime began to weigh upon us. 'We would get into trouble'. A state we particularly dreaded.

We sat around and discussed what to do in a desultory fashion. Eventually it filtered through to us that we would have to turn to some grown-up person and tell them what had happened. Of course in the telling we would ensure that the rest of us would remain entirely blameless. So we put on our dressing gowns and pattered over to the first house in a body to find Matron.

We found her in her usual haunt, which was the linen cupboard. All speaking at once, words rained on her from all directions. Matron gleaned the gist of our story and received our news with due seriousness. When she had quietened us and gathered the relevant details in a reasonable order, she packed us off back to bed and told us to go to sleep.

Once back in bed we couldn't sleep, we were too keyed up, wondering what Miss Meadmore would do when she was told about the runaway. Much later, well into the night, when most had drifted off to sleep, a couple of us were awakened by the sound of an engine. We darted to the window and saw a black taxi stop directly below. In the light from the street lamp we saw Miss Meadmore in her brown outdoor tent, heave herself out of the backdoor of the taxi on to the pavement. Jill followed her. She stood by the front fence as Miss Meadmore paid the driver, looking exactly the same as when we had last seen her. A small silhouette encircled by the halo of lamplight in her school coat and beret, standing upright and still. The two figures turned into the gate and walked slowly up the drive and out of our sight. It was the last time we saw Jill.

The episode was not mentioned the following day and none of the anticipated thrashings took place. We assumed that her father had been sent for and she had been taken home. Much speculation ensued and it was generally agreed it had been a splendid victory. Miss Meadmore was seen as having been routed by superior forces and was in our eyes diminished by the episode. It would never have crossed our minds that perhaps Jill had been asked to leave or (worse still) expelled. We gloated over the scene, quite sure that Jill's irate father had trounced the Meadmores and said all the things we would have loved to say. All about how wicked and cruel they were and how unhappy they had made his 'lovely little girl'.

My grown-up self fears that Jill was probably bundled off in disgrace and never realised that back in the girls' 'dorm' she was the heroine of the hour. For a brief few days she had provided us with what we craved most in the world—a champion. A grown-up person who would stand up to the Meadmores in defence of their child.

Although we were deeply impressed by Jill's action, no one else ever ran away. I knew in my secret heart there would be no point, perhaps the others felt as I did, they could not muster such a champion either.

We had to stand up for ourselves, but I learned a very profound lesson from Jill. She had said 'no'. A little girl, not yet eleven years old, had stepped out all by herself and taken a decision about her own life. It wasn't a rash act brimming with emotion, but calm and considered. She had somewhere else to go that was better, somewhere else she preferred to be. Without any scenes or tantrums or threats, she had simply put on her coat and walked out of the door. I did not think about it clearly or talk about it much, but her behaviour triggered some spring within myself. I was deeply impressed, this was a new and interesting possibility, that you could rationally change a prescribed pattern that had been laid down for you. Although I never copied her, this new dimension broadened my horizon. I became aware of the element of choice in the regulation of peoples lives.

Today this little episode may seem quite commonplace, but I had only ever been surrounded by people for whom living was merely an endurance test.

Winter

The year at The Elms was quite distinctly divided between winter and summer. Most of our childhood skirmishing in the house and garden or park took place in the summer. If not those precise months designated as summer, certainly during the milder softer days of the year.

Winter at school was quite different, winter was a prison. As the temperature gradually dropped so did our spirits and our freedom shrink correspondingly. Winter's grim grey clouds set hard as tombstones until each bright patch of gold and green was totally obliterated.

On late November mornings, when it was my turn to lay the tables for breakfast, the before seven o'clock fog was a smack in the face with a grimy old dish cloth. I tore over to the first house to escape it as soon as possible; to seek refuge in the warm kitchen of bubbling kettles and steaming porage pots.

Everywhere was draughty, the windows rattled, the wind roared up through the bare creaking floorboards and the door hinges whined pitifully. We felt the cold most piercingly in the 'other house'.

For six years my companions and I slept in that huge house with not so much as a candle to warm us. We would go to bed fully dressed with our nighties and dressing gowns over the top of our day clothes. Hugging the couple of thick blankets around our ears and putting our pillows at our backs to keep out the slicing draught from the window, the curtainless windows and bare boards enhanced the unrelenting severity of our surroundings. If by chance you touched the iron bedsteads with a bare arm or wrist the shock of the deathly cold caused a nervous spasm that jerked it away instantaneously. From my bed I watched torrents of rain tearing and tumbling down the gaping window pane. Outside the ivy swayed perilously and juddered against the frames and sills, its long tresses in danger of being torn out by the roots. The trees hammered their sharp nails against the glass and squealed at the pain of the gale, in a desperate attempt to get in and find shelter. Branches, splintered and fractured, hung like broken limbs for weeks until the next rage of winter tore them off completely.

Then the snow came. January of 1947 has never left me. I was seven years old but I can feel it as though it never went away. Like the Snow Queen, I too have fragments of ice lodged in my heart that have never melted in all these years. Lacy frost curtained our windows then, icicles hung huge as stalagmites from gutters and pipes. When, curiously, we snapped bits off freezing needles shot through our hands paralysing them with the intense cold. Burdened with snow, the branches of the elms that lined the furthest fence sagged low enough for me to poke my fingers in as I slithered down to the front gate.

The joy of the park had withered with the leaves. What had been a welcome foray into the outside world, when we took our daily walk, became a dreaded punishment. We would file down to the gate in our usual crocodile and the jagged edges of the razor wind attacked our bare legs mercilessly. The backs of your knees and thighs were raw and chapped for most of the winter and chilblains ached continually. We did not suffer alone, Miss Metcalfe became sere and yellowed by the bitter blow and Miss Polsue's nose grew longer and turned a bluish mauve. Blue veined and peeky under my school hat with my hair scragged back in the institution pigtails, I looked like a skinned rabbit.

One day a beautiful elegant lady took us for our walk. She wore a brown fur coat and had soft curling brown hair to match. When we returned she was quite overcome by the ordeal and swayed delicately against the playroom table. Matron caught her before she fell and called for reviving cups of hot tea for her. I was immensely interested and reflected how wonderful it must be to be grown-up. Many many times I wished someone would want to revive me with cheerful cups of hot tea.

We huddled around the cheerless iron stove in the playroom, trying to draw any breath of warmth from its tepid body.

Those apparently endless stretches of time and space had been rolled up and put away 'until spring'. All we had left was the uncertain shelter of the school building. We felt ourselves more exposed, more vulnerable in such close proximity to the Meadmores. Our smallest gestures and expressions of ourselves as individuals were subject to the severest scrutiny and censure. Cocksure bravado that strutted through our nighttime games subsided into sheepish anxiety. We held our hands behind our backs and fidgeted nervously, reluctant to expose ourselves further.

I sucked my thumb more and more and rocked myself for comfort and twiddled strands of hair or anything else that was close.

Living was chopped up into blocks. Hours spent in the schoolroom, hours spent in the playroom, with the occasional dash across the hall or pelt down the corridor to the kitchen. Mealtimes divided the day and were looked forward to eagerly. The great gash in the day was the hideous walk before tea. I realise now that if we had been more suitably dressed for the weather we would probably have enjoyed it more. Having to be dressed to look like Princess Margaret Rose had considerable disadvantages.

During the confinement of these winter days, we were expected to be in a certain place at a certain time. Any deviation from the programme laid down for us was spotted all too quickly and retribution was swift.

Tightly reined as we were, in our more restricted surroundings we chafed against each other. Cringing timidity did not come naturally to me. I was a born chatterbox and very nosey. It was only the Meadmores' attention I wanted to avoid. During long wet Saturdays, cooped up in the playroom we interfered in each other's games and became restive.

One particular occasion remains crystal clear in my memory. A little boy called Jeremy was studying his stamp collection. None of us had many possessions, so we descended like vultures when anything new appeared. I was picking up his stamps, turning the pages, asking questions and generally making a nuisance of myself. He was a rather studious little boy whose only desire was to be left in peace to pursue his hobby alone. I continued to badger him to swap with me.

Eventually, driven to the end of his patience, he turned quite puce and yelled "Don't be so aggravating".

The sounds of this altercation brought the first Miss Meadmore rampaging into the playroom from the kitchen. She didn't say a word— doors banged, furniture went flying. It was like a tornado hitting the room. She caught me by my hair and dragged me down the corridor, I stumbled about and hit the wall before I hit the floor.

Long spiky splinters embedded themselves in my knees. The corridor seemed ten miles long. When we reached the kitchen she stamped ferociously down every stone step with me walloping every bone of my body on each step. She rammed me behind the back door, where I was left to lick my wounds and consider my crimes for the rest of the afternoon. Jeremy was satisfied and I lost all interest in stamps.

Most of our nastier moments occurred on wet days or foggy days. The trap we fell into was that the great wrath would descend upon us—usually it fell on our hands, with slipper or hairbrush, for apparently trifling reasons. On one occasion I got the hair brush for not changing out of my plimsolls when I popped from one house to another. Yet, when we honestly knew we had been naughty, frequently nothing happened.

The eternity of winter dragged on and sleeping in our clothes and wearing them all day, we became quite mangy. Bathnight was every Saturday and hair washing was in the morning. Apart from these supervised ablutions I hardly ever washed. 'The other house' had no bathroom and on cold mornings I just about ran a comb through my hair, straightened my tunic and pulled my socks up and that was my toilet for the day. Cleaning of teeth was unheard of and my toothbrush remained pristine for years. Only vanity prompted a certain care of ourselves as we grew older.

Our jumpers became horrid and bobbly and our tunics hairy with bedclothes' fluff. We were all smelly together and didn't notice each other. The Meadmores had a combination of warm fat body smell and cats. Our underclothes were changed once a week, which was quite usual for the times. After six days they were hardened by sweat and had thick black rings at the neck and cuffs. The cats didn't like going out in bad weather either and messed or were sick all over the place and the playroom reeked of cat's pee.

Our spirits sank steadily in the smell and the gloom and the misery of the season. The light of the day, forever slate grey, hung in tawdry patches around the house like piles of old rags.

The schoolroom was tightly packed with heavy wooden desks and iron fittings bolted one to the other. There were no aisles. A solid wadge of desks filled the largest area of the room. There was just enough space to walk from the door to the front of the room and another empty gap in the bay of the window. To reach our own desk we had to clamber and crawl along the narrow seats. As we grew older we were permitted to spend some of our evenings and wet or snowy Saturday afternoons in there. We huddled in the bay on the floor to play 'five stones' or marbles and these boinked and rattled on the lumpy floorboards.

Scuffed and scraped by generations of schoolchildren the schoolroom was cramped and sometimes cosy. Scratched wooden planks lined the lower half of the room, and the door and the floorboards that had long ago been stained by a dark varnish looked chewed and gnawed. By daylight half of the room was in a permanent shadow. In our dishevelled navy blue tunics and jumpers we moulded synonymously into our surrounding gloom. We gently melted into the dark brown cupboards walls and floors. A comforting anonymity of bowed heads huddled close to one another. Once bolted in together at our desks any explosive movement or clambering about was a physical impossibility. A pleasant somnolent inertia prevailed. Here, as inmates of winter, we played battleships, or drew ladies in long skirts, or were taught rude words by the boys. On one occasion a supply of lurid American magazines, or rather horror comics, found their way into the schoolroom, probably supplied by 'Stas'. A perfect religious silence reigned as we studied these with our full concentrated attention and digested their content.

Bubblings of sensuality simmered among us, erupting

into odd spurts of giggles and whisperings behind our hands into ears bent low and close to our mouths. Woolly arms curled around each others' shoulders, soft cheeks resting on curly hair, we breathed each other into ourselves. Unfettered by inhibition, this unselfconscious delicate intimacy of childhood was never commented upon and so affectionate impulses blossomed quite naturally. Adults and children were blissfully unsophiscated, no knowing undercurrents existed as they might today. We knew nothing about anything and neither did the Meadmores. When we lolled all over each other, to them, we were no different to their cats; as truly we were not.

Later, at about eleven or twelve, nature prodded us into some acknowledgement of our sex and so we sachéed about, stretching our arms languorously. Coiled around the radiator, the one source of heat, our arms curved around another's waist luxuriating in the warmth, stroking a boy's long eyelashes. He looking coy but we quite unabashed. (Sadly, self-consciousness 'smote us hip and thigh' in the early teens and those sweetly spontaneous gestures were stillborn and hands became clamped to our sides.)

Somewhere deep down within us a bond existed, born of shared experience, that held us close and yet at the same time no real lasting friendships were forged. There were no home visits or exchange of addresses when anyone left. Perhaps it was before the casual social age and we didn't know how to enter into such a relationship. The spiteful pinch of winter was suffered by everyone and so was never spoken about. Our fears, our sorrows, indignities and humiliations, were kept tightly locked inside ourselves. In the absence of parents or any other affectionate adults, having boys around was of quite profound emotional importance. A hand to hold in the crocodile, sometimes a shoulder to rest your head on, someone you chose to sit next to or who sought you out to play with. We were Mum and Dad and child all rolled into one to each other. The term 'boyfriend' was unknown, we needed each other in a way children growing up in families do not. We provided a focus for each other for the tiny buds of feeling that sought some outlet for expression.

This need manifested itself most noticeably in winter. Not only were we physically closer together but all other fields of interest or exploration were impossible, so we turned our attentions inwards to ourselves. Girls were girls and boys were different. A certain instinctive frisson was generated between us and didn't need lessons to perceive that difference. We gleaned the basic facts of nature almost automatically, simply by being together. We knew, without being 'knowing' like Adam and Eve before they were thrown out of Eden. On one occasion good old June and I tied our dressing gowns around us like skirts, fondly imagining we looked like Dorothy Lamour and 'hula hulaed' for the boys as they queued for the toilet on the bench below the stairs before they went to bed. This entertainment was greeted by appreciative sniggers and hisses.

'Wobin Wobinson' kissed me under the table in the playroom. John was always rather dour and disapproved of such carryings on. While Andrew just grinned and happily allowed the girls to be 'soppy' over him sometimes. It was very light and cheerful. Stas and Andreas practised their Mediterranean charm on us and saucy smiles shone out of those bug brown eyes.

Generally we co-existed amicably and I genuinely did not know how cruel and unkind children could be to each other until I went to day school.

Of course we squabbled and bickered from time to time and spontaneous outbursts would occur over games, but it was superficial and short lived. Perhaps we were too young or had never learned from older brothers and sisters, but I have no recollection of any 'ganging up' or calculated acts of unkindness.

All those winters are squashed into each other like soggy tomato sandwiches. They dragged their way from crisp iciness and razor-edged winds into dank muddy spring. A kind of airless musty exhaustion laid us low with a heavy lethargy. No spurts of intrigue or quirks of fancy quickened our spirits or kindled our energies. Smelly 'cats' lingered in our nostrils.

Then it seemed one day the wind softened into a breeze, our bodies moved more freely and once more we were welcomed into a green and pretty land. In the garden the trees were in bud and tiny shoots poked through brown soil like buried treasure waiting to be found. Silver sunlight dazzled us as our cases were laid out on the dining room tables and we waited, hovering around the clock, to be collected and taken home for the holidays.

A Park and a Garden

Jill had not been an obviously rebellious child and neither was I. There were many aspects of school life I really enjoyed. But I had recognised that, within my limitations, I too inwardly rejected much of what the school represented. I resented the snobbery, the violence, and the austerity of the Meadmores' regime. I never talked about it because I didn't truly believe that my situation could be improved. I knew my mother was doing the best she could for me in the circumstances. My mother endured her life and she couldn't cope without me enduring it with her.

I trundled along from year to year, growing up without realising, remaining fairly separate and apart from most adults. In this way my deepest and most abiding relationship was with nature. The garden of the two houses and Grange Park, which across the road opposite the school, was where we children were happiest. We strayed into the garden in almost any weather, if we were supposed to be there or not, and we were taken to the park each day for our daily walk.

The stern authority of the Meadmores did not seem to extend beyond the walls of the first house. Every day after lessons and before tea we would put on our berets and coats and form up in our little jiggling crocodile. Two by two like Noah's flock we crossed the road feeling horribly conspicuous and open to the public gaze. Once inside the park Miss Metcalfe was always noticeably cheerier and even sad. Miss Polsue managed a crack of a smile on these little forays into the outside world.

We entered through a side gate, past the boys' High School and into a very wide, very long avenue of trees. They stood straight and tall, regularly spaced like temple columns, their leafy canopies over arching, almost entwining a beautiful vaulted cathedral of an avenue. It was a triumphal walk way through the park. On either side grassland rolled away as far as you could see. Sometimes we saw red squirrels scampering along the roots, helter skeltering up the trunks to disappear in the dense foliage. Dogs sprinted, their legs full stretched, joyous at the great freedom of such space. Our spirits raced with them. Half way down the avenue we turned on to a path that led up a grassy slope, a long slow incline, into the wide open grassland of the park. Once at the top of the hillock you could look around you and see for what seemed like miles. Here and there were gracefully posed clumps of trees elegantly extending their branches to the sky.

Everywhere was alive and springy and crowded with scurrying busy creatures. Flurries of birds swept from the trees twittering and cawing as they swirled around in their unending games of tag. The wind raced across the grass, tickling the leaves snatching our berets, hurly-burlying upwards to dance among the high treetops. Tugging the boughs this way and that, uncertain which way to go, finally flinging itself up into the piled pillows of the clouds.

Miss Metcalfe spread her small blanket over the roots at the base of a wide sheltering trunk of an oak. We sped away from her carried on the wind like scraps of paper. Swooping and shrieking hither and thither. Falling to the ground into a wild exultant roly poly down the grassy slope, to land in a tangled heap at the bottom. Then jumping up again to scramble back up the hill and do it all over again. Eventually, when we were exhausted, we came back to Miss Metcalfe and all tried to sit on the tiny blanket until poor Miss Metcalfe was almost smothered and protested at our treatment of her.

Once the wildness in us had had full expression we settled to quieter more industrious pursuits. The busy life of the park caught our attention and we collected pretty coloured leaves or twigs or berries and conkers, according to the season. Hiding our treasures in the deep roots of the trees, leaving little stores of nuts for the squirrels to find. Other times we stalked the grasshoppers and watched the ants seeking their highways, measuring how far they travelled. All nature was of consuming interest to us for we had no distractions, no television, radio, toys, few books or organised games. We had only what the earth provided for our stimulation and entertainment. We knew where the birds nested and where the stag beetles lurked. We combed the grass to see how many different kinds we could collect. We put the buttercups under our chins; if the yellow glowed on our skin then we liked butter. Miss Polsue would be garlanded with daisy chains that we sat and made with endless patience. Posies of wild flowers were taken back to school and carefully pressed in dictionaries and forgotten. To be rediscovered months later with delight. The boys made slings and catapults from twigs and the elastic that held up our socks. Fallen branches were staves and spears for war games and being Robin Hood's merry men. Piles of stones would be heaped up for the camp fires of Cowboys and Indians.

The only time we didn't want to go out was when it was bitterly cold and the sharp wind whisked cruelly around the backs of our legs leaving them chafed and sore. At these times our bedraggled crocodile perambulated sadly around the park and back to school again without stopping.

On one occasion we were taken out by someone else, a lady we had never seen before and ventured further into a new and hitherto uncharted area of the park. We came upon an old disused open-air theatre. It was a yellow grey November day and the mist crept up menacingly from the stream. Stale milky streaks of clammy fog hung low over the grass, the reeds and bushes. When we separated we became invisible to each other. I clambered up on to the rotting boards of the stage, curious to know what was beyond the platform. The ancient flats leaned drunkenly, decayed, smelling rotten, the boards under my feet limp and soggy, shifted under my tread. Filthy cotton straggled down to the floor from the proscenium that sagged in a V-shape tattered with strips of mouldy paper. Old cardboard boxes and leaves stinking and congealed were heaped about the stage.

The whole place reeked of death and as I nosed around among the rubble the greasy mist clung to me like weed. I was reminded of the little mermaid when she made her perilous journey to the sea witch, to beg to be made human. Heavy globs of water fell like stones on to my head and shoulders from the mouldering structure above. I looked out into the ghastly dank mist that threatened to envelop me, freezing inside my clothes with the fear and isolation of the place.

At last I heard the others calling, strange unearthly cries and I scrambled down to follow in the direction of the sounds. After my glimpse of that foul wilderness of death the hard bare boards of the crowded noisy playroom seemed the most welcoming cheerful place on earth.

I saw the little theatre once again some time later, in the slanting pale light of an insipid afternoon. Stripped of its ghostly aura it looked wretched and sad. None of us wanted to play there, it evoked no magic, it was a dead place, it didn't belong in the park.

On Sundays the park was quite different. In the particular spot to which we were usually taken, lots of people gathered to fly kites and model aeroplanes. They huddled in little concentrated groups, fiddling and twiddling with their precious machinery. Our boys hovered near them, hands in pockets, necks craning, but anxious not to venture too close or appear too familiar. A friendly buzzing sound filled the air, the atmosphere was festive like a bank holiday. The little families or groups of young men played happily and talked and laughed together. It was pleasant to be with them and feel part of the gathering, but we never joined anyone or spoke to them. We were not the same, we were outside that kind of life. A collective diffidence kept us on the edge, watching, as though on the other side of a window.

During term time the park was our only contact with the outside world, apart from the occasional visits from parents or other relations. We knew nothing of the rows of streets neighbouring the school. I recognised that the houses were nothing like the houses where I lived, but I never thought about the people living in them. They were just houses, another part of the landscape. It was only in the park that we saw people and they were strangers, as everyone in this place that we lived, was a stranger. Occasionally we saw big boys in the bright blue blazers of the High School carrying small brown cases, kicking a ball about or throwing thick sticks up into the trees. Ladies in headscarves walked their dogs and elderly couples strolled arm in arm with shopping bags.

We had no idea of the locality beyond the walk to the park, the walk to church and the walk to Carshalton, a matter of perhaps half a mile radius. Even in this short distance we had no idea of where the turnings along the way led, or how the roads interconnected.

Seasons came and went and we plotted their course, spotting each new bud and leaf close to the ground, closer to nature and all its living things. Chunks of poetry were given to us to learn and they weren't just words on a page— daffodils, swaying grass and racing clouds. They were real. This was our world, more real to us than anything else. The sparseness of our lives indoors made us doubly aware of the abundance and richness of the park and garden. Nearly all our little treasures were gleaned from the park. Tiny acorn men, their cups turned into hats sitting on twigs adorned the mantelpiece of the 'dorm'. Special stones, the right size and weight, were used as 'five stones' and snails were smuggled in and kept as pets in our desks. Of course they were discovered because we felt it necessary to feed them on greens from our dinner. The Meadmores were horrified. There were good thrashings all round and they were unceremoniously thrown away.

All kinds of other illicit pets were kept. In the garden outside the other house was an ancient and abandoned greenhouse with several panes missing and clogged with old earth. The occasional bird that had been injured was carefully tended in the greenhouse. Worm collecting expeditions were organised to try to keep them alive. Sadly the poor things always died in spite, or perhaps because of, our ministrations. While they were alive we took turns at keeping a vigil with our patient, who was kept trapped in what we fondly imagined was a suitable nest of leaves and grass in an old seed box. It was pitiful to watch their scrabblings becoming more feeble each day. Finally they were wrapped in stiff toilet paper and buried under the hedge. After a few years we had quite a little cemetery. Those fearful cats had a lot to answer for.

The garden had three quite separate areas. At the bottom

of the steps that led up to the French windows of the dining room was a perfect square of bright green lawn. This was bordered by a thin strip of small flowers and shrubs on every side. Behind the flowers a high trellis was thickly covered by a mass of rambling roses. I never saw anyone, child or teacher ever set foot in the rose garden, but it did provide a very pleasing outlook from the dining room. A gardener came regularly and diligently attended to the lawn and roses. To one side of the trellis was the wooden hall and beyond was the playground. This had once been grass too, but generations of feet had trampled it into total baldness. Just here and there was a brave tuft or two of grass. To one side a stocky oak tree stood with thickly spreading branches. Here we ran about and jumped or sat under the protective foliage at appointed times of the day. If we had particularly exasperated the Meadmores beyond endurance, the entire school would run around the perimeter for several laps. Even between them they did not have the strength to spank us all.

One summer a rubber paddling pool appeared, filled with water and we were permitted to put on our bathing suits and take turns splashing about. It soon became filled with leaves and the water grew very murky. This was diverting for a little while, but usually the playground was not a popular haunt, it was too exposed to the attention of the Meadmores for us to want to linger on its uninspiring baldness.

Beyond the vegetable patch, behind the playground, low bushes and trees huddled together and in the centre of this rather unruly heart of the garden was a small pond. This pond was forgotten and overlooked, overgrown, weed-choked, left to moulder like an old lost plimsoll. Guarded closely by the generous branches of an old low apple tree it was almost completely hidden from view. It was a place I liked to be. I used to creep through the bushes from time to time and lean over scraping my knees on the cement sides. Sometimes the water lily pads almost covered the entire surface of the water and were so green. Occasionally the frogs would obligingly hop about on the leaves to entertain me. When the flowers bloomed there was something so immaculate about the way they were arranged, like cups and saucers on a dinner table, their wonderfully rounded petals perfectly curved into ice cream dollops. I liked to look at the pond and watch the activity in the watery world, poking the leaves, mesmerising myself with the infinite variation of the ripples and patterns in the water. It was the marvellous freedom of the park and the garden that attracted me. Both home and school were places of restraint and constraint where you had to be on your guard, always ready to fend off fresh onslaughts of criticism and judgement. But once outside the door, outside the walls, those fetters fell away from me. The wind blew far and wide across the open land and it seemed to take me with it. My heart and my spirit lifted with the leaves and I felt a part of everything.

Retribution and Revenge

I might have trotted meekly into The Elms as trusting as a lamb, but I certainly didn't leave like one. By the time I was eleven I wasn't quite the oldest member of the girls 'dorm', but I was one of the most 'experienced'. Without particularly meaning to I had slipped into Denise's shoes. I was less vociferous than she had been, but in many ways I was more reckless. This proved to be my undoing. Perhaps I too was afflicted by the 'leaving soon' syndrome. We wanted to do something that we hadn't done before and after nearly six years there wasn't much left.

Nearly all our escapades in some way involved food and apart from the secret passages episode were born from a moment of sudden inspiration. This was no different. It was one of those in between times. It wasn't properly summer and it wasn't really spring. One of those typically English nothing sort of times. The evening was dull for long enough after we were dispatched to bed for us to be up and around fidgeting in our rooms. We had rearranged our drawers for the umpteenth time and investigated and reinvestigated our few possessions. We had run in and out of each other's rooms, teased Mavis and irritated those blessed souls who wished to sleep. The evening had slipped into night without us realising it and still we were as lively as ants in an anthill.

One of us, probably emerging fresh from the forbidden pages of the *Girls Crystal,* mentioned something about a Midnight Feast. We were just in the right frame of mind to be properly receptive to the idea. At the same time it didn't generate quite the usual current of powerful imaginative thrill among us, It was a good workmanlike idea and as such had to be tackled in a similar manner. There was no problem about getting the food or where the event should take place. It had to be held in the bedroom, these things always were. Also it wasn't quite warm enough to be ferreting about in the garden.

A small raiding party got dressed and prepared for an assault on the cellar under the kitchen in the main house. There was an entrance to the cellar in the back garden, well obscured by the flight of stone steps that led to the French windows of the dining room. I say an entrance because there was no real door— it was an opening, like the opening to a cave. Large quantities of potatoes and vegetables were delivered here and stacked in sacks deep inside. At this furthest end were some rickety wooden steps that led up to the kitchen. The 'store' room, as it was called, also had a satisfying smell of old sacks, onions, and earth. It was quite dry and any wind there was, whisked around like a feather duster, keeping the goods well aired and cool.

Once long ago, the brick walls had been painted with white distemper and although now greyish and flaking, with bald spots where they were most bumped and scraped, it afforded just enough light to break the dense blackness. A grey backwash of light from the entrance was bolstered by the once white walls.

We naughty little girls pitter-pattered between the sacks and boxes. We knew what we were doing was wrong. This wasn't an adventure where we swept along without fully realising what the outcome would be, when we were overtaken by a compulsion to test ourselves or satisfy our curiosity. This was an act of deliberate and calculated villainy. We intended to raid the school supplies. It was also an act of crass stupidity. Did I really think no one would notice? The answer is 'Yes I did'.

A little bit from this sack another bit from that box, a tin, a packet here and there. Like rats we scavenged, nibbled and gnawed into cardboard boxes and netting bags. With almost total disregard for what we collected, or the debris we left behind, we stuffed our hoard into pillow cases and trooped back to our rooms triumphant in our wickedness. Heedless of rationing and carefully considered food requirements for the whole school for the weeks to come— a kind of dreadful resentful bravado burned within us. It was ours anyway wasn't it? Our food. Who had paid for it anyway? None of us that was sure. Once we were back in our rooms we tipped our stolen goodies out on to the beds. Some girls must have gone right up the stairs into the kitchen, because among the extraordinary selection of foodstuffs were several rashers of bacon, some butter and a nearly empty jar of jam.

Rather like feeding the five thousand, we dished out our odd array, willy nilly, without much consideration for what might naturally go with what. This resulted in some sickening concoctions. Sickening to me now that is— at the time I was quite oblivious of their eccentricity. June happily spread butter on her cornflakes, or Post Toasties it might have been, as if it was the most natural thing in the world. Bacon of course has to be cooked, this was no problem to us juvenile commandos. After all there was a fireplace in our room, so what was more natural than that we should light a fire? Someone was dispatched to the garden to fetch a few twigs or bits of wood and June and I sneaked into Matron's room.

Now is the time to confess that we had done this many times before. Matron had a much coveted gas fire in her room and in the interminable winter nights, when we couldn't sleep and were miserable with cold, we would creep in and have a warm in front of it. By some wonderful stroke of good fortune she always kept a box of matches on the mantelpiece, which was most considerate of her. So having a fry up was a relatively simple matter.

Among our peculiar assortment of goods was a couple of tins of sardines which happily had little keys with which to open them. We scooped out the sardines and carefully laid them aside on a comic. Now we had two little frying pots. Once our wood was merrily blazing away we ripped the bacon into little bits and cut up the potato with a nail file. We were so happy and pleased with ourselves we nearly burst at the unexpected success of our venture.

This was really living! Our bacon sizzled marvellously and spat fat and sardine oil in all directions. Flames spurted wildly, it was wonderful. Five wicked little faces glowed with delight. When we were satisfied they were more or less cooked we dragged the tins out of the mess of burning twigs with pencils, scattering cinders and sparks even further over the wooden floor. There was no real grate, our joyous blaze was on the stone floor of the fireplace. By some miracle we didn't set anything else on fire, but not for want of trying. The twigs crackled and banged and smoked appallingly but we didn't mind at all. I'm sure if the whole room had gone up in flames we'd have been even more ecstatic.

We chewed on our half cooked bits of bacon and potatoes and wiped our greasy mouths with grimy fingers. With the backs of our hands we smeared our smoke-blackened moustaches even further over our faces and with ultimate fulfilment rubbed our hands on our wincy nightdresses, grinning dreadfully at each other. What a feast it had been! It was rounded off with a piece of apple each, cornflakes, butter, jam and sardines. We all agreed it was the best food we had ever tasted in our whole lives.

Mercifully the twigs finally burned themselves out and saved us from total extinction. A messy little pile of ashes and half burned stumps remained. When they were cool enough to touch we scooped them up on comics and flushed them down the lavatory. Our hearts and tummies being completely satisfied we rolled our dirty little selves into bed.

Once an occasion is over and done with it is very difficult to conceive that it can be dragged back from its rightful place in the past. It is as though something has returned from the dead. To be caught in the act was what we always expected and dreaded, which was why most of our escapades were hurried excited affairs. We usually raced through an adventure anxious to reach the final haven and safety of our beds. This being done, then it was all right, we had got away with it again.

'We have got away with it' was precisely the emotion that lulled us contentedly to sleep that night. Again we had got away with it, we had triumphed over our captors, we had run rings around them. Like clever little mice we scurried about and the big fat cats couldn't catch us. So the following morning as we pushed and shoved in the breakfast line it came as a double shock when all the older girls were summoned by the first Miss Meadmore.

The Meadmores were always swift in their vengeance and that day was to be no different. We were ushered into the ghastly inner sanctum of the cold, blue, beautiful lounge. Shuffling and shrinking against each other, desperately trying to remain as close to the door as possible, praying to be struck by invisibility as flight was out of the question, we waited for the inevitable. All those little faces looked bilious and cadaverous with fear. We knew we would be thrashed, that wasn't the shock. It was like an axe splitting your head open. It wasn't the thrashing, though God knows, that was bad enough. The worst part was that 'They knew'. We had been found out! 'They' knew. 'They' knew that we got up to little tricks at night. If I'd fallen down to the bottom of a well I couldn't have felt worse. The whole kit and caboodle for our survival and existence at The Elms had been smashed to smithereens. 'They' knew something terribly personal and private about us. We had been deshelled like snails and our delicate soft inner selves were raw, silently screaming for a place to crawl into.

Both the Meadmores were in the lounge. The second Miss Meadmore must have considered the matter of earth-shattering importance and risen at dawn in order to make the perilous descent of the stairs, and be ensconced in a huge armchair by nine thirty. Her presence added weight (if you'll pardon the expression) and majesty to the occasion. Like Queen Victoria she was not amused and her brown eyes turned jet black as she pierced our very souls. The first Meadmore, her bulk firmly mastered, stood as solid as rock on two legs widespread. A Colossus in a flowery apron, one massive hand on one massive hip. Her face was vermilion streaked with puce and the white cotton wool hair wobbled with fury.

Few words were spoken, no time was wasted. Ringleaders were selected for a very special thrashing on our bare bottoms as well as our hands. Inevitably and jus-tifiably I was chosen for this extra special attention. I am sure what I felt must be similar to those about to be hanged or shot. Terror and shock makes you cold and you shake. Try as you might you can't stop, you can't do anything but obey automatically. All personal will vanishes as though it never existed, no part of your body obeys you.

'Bend over'—you bend.

Scratching talons strong as steel tear your clothes away from you. The other claw grips your neck, pressing your head down further and further. Bang, bang, bang, bang, bang, bang. A wide wood-backed hairbrush beats you rhythmically like a giant driving in a stake.

'Stand up'—you stand, your clothes in a twisted heap somewhere around you.

'Hold out your hand'—you put out your hand, straight and stretched, tight and taut.

Your fingers bent back as far as they will go so your palm is stiff as bamboo in a final agonising effort at self control.

All in vain, your fingers are snatched and squeezed like plasticine. Bang, bang, bang, bang, bang, bang, down comes the mallet all over again.

Then strangely it's over. No one speaks. You leave the room and go to the lavatory. Why is it always the lavatory? I don't suppose the gentleman who invented them ever realised that they would take over from the church as the only final sanctuary of the fugitive from life's agonies.

Well that was it, it was all over. No one knew how 'They' found out. It is fairly obvious now—the wreckage we must have left in the storeroom or perhaps even the smoke from the fire. When our bodies and our minds had recovered enough to discuss the unhappy incident, we all agreed to lie low and lead quiet lives for a long while. But children quickly forget, remarkably quickly or at least apparently, forget. We'd been naughty and we'd paid the price. We felt no more than our usual bitter hatred towards the first Miss Meadmore. No one even suggested putting rat poison in her tea. Deep down we appreciated it was 'a fair cop'. That being so, the episode was closed.

The school had a Brownie pack attached to it and naturally as recreation and entertainment were scarce the girls were all enthusiastic members. Our uniforms were highly prized and carefully looked after and we enjoyed the weekly meetings in the draughty wooden hall where we played games and performed mysterious rites with toadstools. Very occasionally in the summer we were permitted to go 'tracking' in the park, an event that created high excitement and even more rarely we attended mass Brownie and Guide occasions when we actually left the school and were taken on buses to other venues where we had buns and orange squash. There were definite advantages to being members of the Brownies.

I was a sixer, a position of unimaginable superiority with an armful of badges that weighed me down like campaign medals. My only minor irritation was that I was a gnome and I secretly hankered to be a fairy. Many hours were whiled away sewing on badges perfectly, tying our ties, fiddling about with our belts, worrying that our uniforms were too short. Because these uniforms were not new but inherited from previous generations of Elms' Brownies.

The following week after the 'shameful episode' we had a meeting as usual and we all bounced in eagerly, ready for fun and games and more badges and sitting on the toadstool and all the usual pantomime. But we were not to be in the hall as usual. Nothing about the evening was as usual. Brown Owl led her exuberant charges over to the other house and we were directed into one of the deserted and abandoned rooms on the ground floor. The enormous windows gaped with cold insipid sunlight. Brown Owl called for us all to stand in a line. It seemed strange but we did as we were bid. After we'd fiddled ourselves into convenient positions, changing places several times of course before this was achieved, a curious lull spread through our ranks.

And then it happened. Brown Owl asked me to step forward, which I did without question, having no idea what she intended. I stood facing the line of neatly uniformed pale soft-skinned Brownies. Brown Owl stood behind me. Her actual words meant nothing and not one do I recall. Instead it was like being hit silently on the head from behind. Somewhere above and behind me my recent crimes fell down upon my ears. I had opened a door of a booby trapped cupboard and tin cans and buckets of water rained upon my head. Like a stopped clock everything about me was stuck in the same position.

Nice, kindly dear Brown Owl continued to deliver her execution speech and just the tail end dripped sickly into my head.

"...and you will not be allowed to fly up to the Guides."

Then from her capacious pocket that lay upon her capacious breasts, she produced a small pair of curved scissors and with meticulous precision she snip, snip, snipped at the stitches on my prized sixer's stripes. This tiny physical snipping action prodded me into some kind of response. The expression slid off my face, falling down to somewhere around my navel.

"I don't care, you can keep your bloody stupid Guides", I snarled to myself resentfully.

I had been drummed out of the Brownies— cashiered. It was not quite a drumhead court martial, as I was given no chance to defend myself. This made no difference because I was as guilty as hell anyway.

Before this dramatic episode I felt I had sinned fairly dreadfully, been statutorily thrashed and paid my debt to society. Standing there before the slightly dazed faces of the other Brownies, I felt more defenceless than I had ever been at any time. They couldn't look at me, embarrassed by the situation and at the same time relieved and innocent of any participation in the crime. They were totally exonerated because hadn't Brown Owl said that I 'was the Sixer'—? I 'was the Leader'. I 'should have known better'. All their guilt was now comfortably lifted from their shoulders and pressed down painfully upon me. I was the outcast, the scapegoat.

So it seemed it was my fate to end my days at The Elms in fairly well deserved ignominy. However there was to be one more totally unexpected twist in the tail or tale.

Some months previously I had taken my eleven plus exam. A strange ordeal involving me being given my bus fare to Mitchum Girl's High School plus some rudimentary directions as to how to get there. By some miracle I didn't get lost and found myself stumbling about what seemed to be acres of rockeries. A kindly older girl plucked me from the abundant foliage and shepherded me to a frighteningly large building. She took me to a big room with long plastic-topped tables, where there were several other older girls, who were so nice they seemed like smiling kindly angels from Heaven. I had been furnished with a few sandwiches and here in this room I was apparently to eat my lunch. One of them showed me pictures of Koala bears. It was all very strange and bewildering. I was almost incapable of uttering a sound. It was as though I had shrunk and everything was happening miles above my head. The voices, the smiles, the laughter all floated down to me as if I had died and had no part in the proceedings.

Those same smiling faces and kindly hands led me to an enormous hall, where, in company with hundreds of other girls, I was to sit the examination. I don't remember another thing. I suppose when it was over I must have found my way back to the bus and The Elms. The whole experience had been so disorienting and alarming that I was anxious to forget all about it.

The Meadmores were predictably pessimistic about my

chances of success and had conveyed this information to my mother. She must have shared their opinion because plans were made for me to go to the local Clarks College in Walthamstow.

Well, one day, very close to my last days of disgrace at The Elms, I was summoned to the lounge. My heart stopped as usual with gut-wrenching apprehension. What was I in trouble for this time?

The first Miss Meadmore was standing in the bay window, looking hideously benign. Suddenly I became 'My dear' I was invited to move closer. Deeply suspicious, I barely moved. She gestured towards me waving a piece of paper and grunts and disconnected words came out of her mouth Of course she would be so pleased and proud to tell my mother.

Evidently I had passed the scholarship. I couldn't believe it, I just couldn't believe it. I had won a place at the Grammar School. Failure was what I had been superbly prepared for. My future school life had been comfortably settled and now I was thrown into confusion once again. I stood there stupidly not knowing what to say.

Slowly the information sank into my bread pudding brain and a marvellous glee spread through my whole being. It wasn't pride that I felt, it was a dreadful gloating satisfaction. Somehow in the last round I had won on points. Now I was fêted and held up as a model pupil. I enjoyed my brief moment of triumph, then I was gone, my six years at The Elms preparatory school were over.

The Elms was a very curious place, so curious that it did eventually make a small item on the front pages of the *Daily Express*—something about 'shock-horror' concerning hygiene, general conditions and so many cats. It was about three years after I had left. Nanny and my mother expressed a passing interest and moved on to the next page and that was how my whole experience of those years was viewed by most of the family. It was a minor episode of minor interest, and I just passed on to the rest of my life.

At first I would mention the odd Elms' incident at my new school, but I soon stopped doing so because it accentuated my difference from my fellows. There was quite enough that made me different already. My mother had married again so her name was not the same as mine anymore. Also I did not live with her, I had stayed at Lime Street to placate Nanny.

All this was quite sufficiently complicated for teachers and classmates to comprehend, without aggravating the situation by regurgitating quaint little stories of a mysterious boarding school. I let it fall behind me, it was much more important to be one of the girls at my new grammar school. I settled down after a while and made good friends who helped me to adjust to my new life.

Although you realise that the edges of memory have dissolved and the exactly accurate picture exists no more, the emotional memory is true and astonishingly clear. Those initial reactions are the scraps that are left to be pieced together and finally comes understanding.

All of us are the playthings of circumstance, not only ourselves, but those responsible for us, often called upon to make far reaching decisions on the turn of a card or in a moment of frailty. In those cheerless, miserable years of the late forties and early fifties, it was the war that was the common denominator in everyone's lives. Some families were more shattered by it than others, but no one was left untouched.

To me Walthamstow and Lime Street was one derelict bomb site where everything was rationed, most of all happiness. The oppressive drabness and dreariness was, for a child worse than the cosy violence of the war which had been important and significant. I inherited the peace which was sour and barren. The Elms was an introduction to a gentler and sweeter landscape.

Walking back along those long corridors of childhood, seeing once again the shadows lying sleek and black as the night settled in upon us, I can see such an ordinary child. A child who was often lonely and fearful, nervously obedient to the power wielded by adults, who secretly suspected she had been 'sent away'. A secret too awful to be allowed any shape or form, that merely trembled like a leaf withering on a bow almost ready to fall. I felt myself to be unworthy to be permitted to remain with my mother. I was too noisy, too strident, too physically troublesome for her. And the echoes that tumble down from so many directions and resonate and reverberate as one yawning sound leaps upon another, is not a discordant note that is left winnowing forever into the distance.

For I accepted my fears and insecurity and learned to keep them within a childish buoyancy. They merely pricked, irritatingly, inside a wilful and at times reckless nature. A defiant strength grew in me. I was proud of my escapades. I had withstood The Elms and it gave me strength to stand up to other things in my life, even though, at the same time, I was terrified by what retribution I might bring down upon my head. I was often afraid but I was never cowed.

So many tears, enough to make a desert bloom, but also a certainty that though I may not like it, if I had to, I could manage on my own. For I knew no one was ever really alone and when I watched the rain trickle down the window pane and heard the wind sighing in the trees, fingered the icicles and wondered at the boughs so heavy with snow, I knew I was part of all that. I was a part of this world, wrapped around by the great elms that led down to the gate, nourished by the lilies that floated gently on the pond, the exuberant roses, gooseberries, birds and hedgehogs.

I grew up in a garden flattened by the storm, withering in the winter, but eager for fresh life each spring, always ready to bloom again in the summer sun.